AIM Higher!

FCAT Mathematics Review

Level C

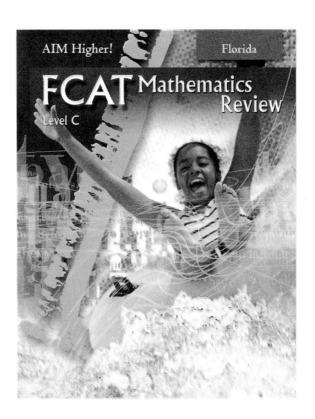

Diane Perkins Castro
and Mark Roop-Kharasch

aim higher!®
Great Source Education Group
Wilmington, MA

Editorial

Diane Perkins Castro
Mark Roop-Kharasch
Robert D. Shepherd
Barbara R. Stratton

Consultants

Todd Bersaglieri*
Matthew Beyranevand*
Sheri Ann Cheng*
Annie Sun Choi‡
Rosalie Fazio§
Sharon Greenwald§
Sylvia D. Leonard*
Matt Stuck*

* *Mathematics Teacher*
‡ *Mathematics Editor*
§ *Mathematics Teacher/Facilitator*

Design & Production

Paige Larkin
Marie Anne E. St. Arnaud

aim higher! More than just teaching to the test™

First Edition

Printed in the United States of America

1 2 3 4 5 6 7 8 9 10 DBH 08 07 06 05 04

International Standard Book Number: 1-58171-387-8

CONTENTS

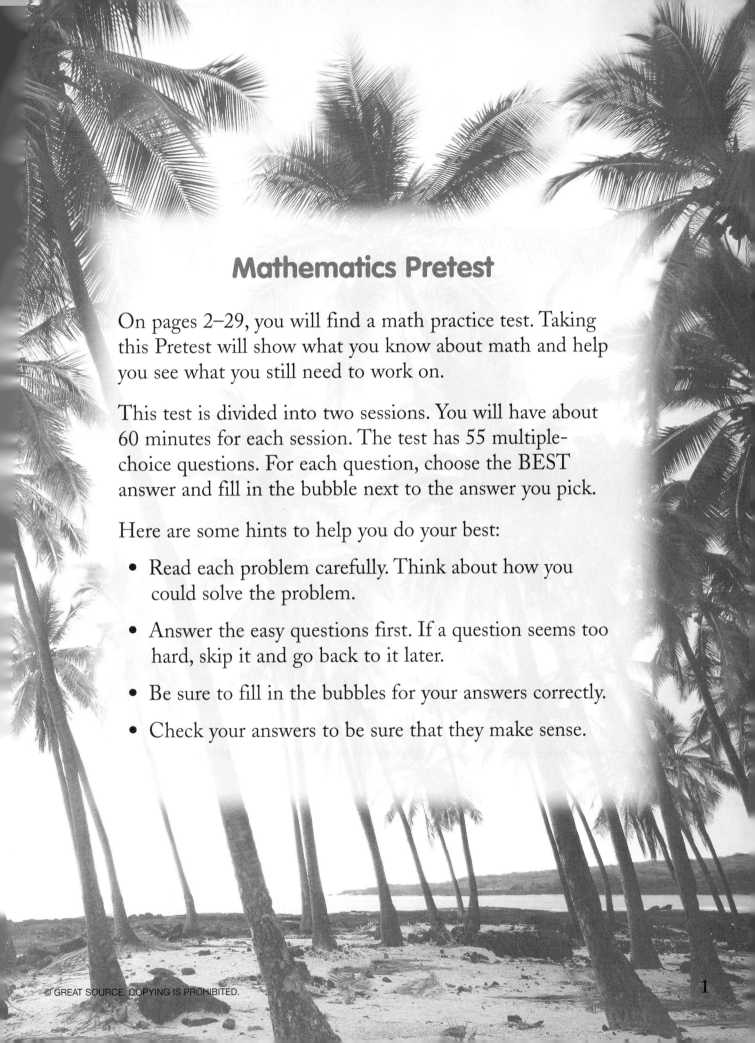

Mathematics Pretest

On pages 2–29, you will find a math practice test. Taking this Pretest will show what you know about math and help you see what you still need to work on.

This test is divided into two sessions. You will have about 60 minutes for each session. The test has 55 multiple-choice questions. For each question, choose the BEST answer and fill in the bubble next to the answer you pick.

Here are some hints to help you do your best:

- Read each problem carefully. Think about how you could solve the problem.

- Answer the easy questions first. If a question seems too hard, skip it and go back to it later.

- Be sure to fill in the bubbles for your answers correctly.

- Check your answers to be sure that they make sense.

Name _____   Class _____   Date _____

MATHEMATICS PRETEST

Directions: *There are 27 multiple-choice questions in this session. For each question, choose the best answer and mark your choice in the book.*

1. There are 9 puppies in the pet shop window. Some puppies are sleeping, and some are eating. There are **twice as many** puppies sleeping as eating. How many puppies are doing each activity?

   Ⓐ 8 sleeping, 1 eating

   Ⓑ 7 sleeping, 2 eating

   Ⓒ 6 sleeping, 3 eating

   Ⓓ 5 sleeping, 4 eating

2. Which of these figures has $\frac{1}{4}$ shaded?

   Ⓐ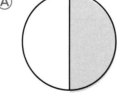

   Ⓒ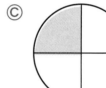

   Ⓑ

   Ⓓ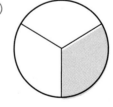

2   **AIM Higher! FCAT Mathematics**

3. Jaime is baking cookies for 7 friends. Jaime will give the same number of cookies to each friend. Which of the following could be the number of cookies that Jaime is baking?

Ⓐ   9 cookies

Ⓑ 17 cookies

Ⓒ 27 cookies

Ⓓ 28 cookies

4. Mr. Mantas is mailing a glass bowl in a rectangular box. He wants the Post Office to be careful with the box. He puts a sticker on **every side** of the box, including the top and bottom, to warn people to be careful. How many stickers does he use?

Ⓐ 4 stickers

Ⓑ 5 stickers

Ⓒ 6 stickers

Ⓓ 7 stickers

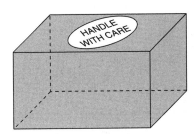

5. Between which two numbers does **476** go?

Ⓐ between 198 and 328

Ⓑ between 239 and 378

Ⓒ between 294 and 501

Ⓓ between 544 and 676

6. Look at the grid below. Which battleship is found at point **(3, 7)**?

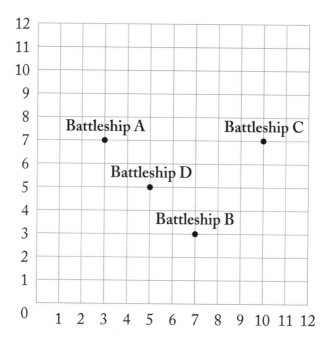

Ⓐ Battleship A

Ⓑ Battleship B

Ⓒ Battleship C

Ⓓ Battleship D

7. Kayla knows that her fingertip is about 1 centimeter (cm) wide. She is measuring the length of a toy car.

1 cm

Which of the following is closest to the length of the toy car?

Ⓐ 4 cm

Ⓑ 5 cm

Ⓒ 6 cm

Ⓓ 7 cm

8. If Arturo spins this spinner many times, which number will the spinner probably land on **least** often?

Ⓐ 1

Ⓑ 2

Ⓒ 3

Ⓓ 4

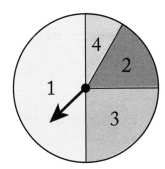

Go On

9. What is the **area** of the shaded figure?

    Ⓐ 7 squares

    Ⓑ 8 squares

    Ⓒ $8\frac{1}{2}$ squares

    Ⓓ 9 squares

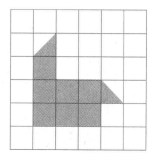

10. In which group below are all three figures **symmetrical**?

Ⓐ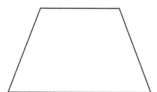

Ⓑ

Ⓒ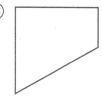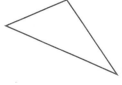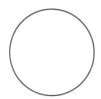

Ⓓ

11. Matthew built a tower of blocks that was 23 inches tall. Erica built a tower of blocks that was **twice as tall** as Matthew's tower. How tall was Erica's tower?

Ⓐ 25 in.

Ⓑ 46 in.

Ⓒ 47 in.

Ⓓ 56 in.

12. Which would be the **best** unit to use to measure the length of your arm?

Ⓐ millimeters

Ⓑ centimeters

Ⓒ meters

Ⓓ kilometers

Go On

13. Mrs. Alvarez coaches a girls' indoor soccer team. She made a list of the number of goals each girl scored during the season. What is the **mode** from this list?

Ⓐ 2 goals

Ⓑ 3 goals

Ⓒ 7 goals

Ⓓ 9 goals

Goals Scored: 2, 2, 2, 3, 5, 6, 9

14. Using the list above, what is the **range**?

Ⓐ 2 goals

Ⓑ 3 goals

Ⓒ 7 goals

Ⓓ 9 goals

15. The graph shows how many baseball gloves Champion Sports Store sold during one week.

BASEBALL GLOVES SOLD THIS WEEK

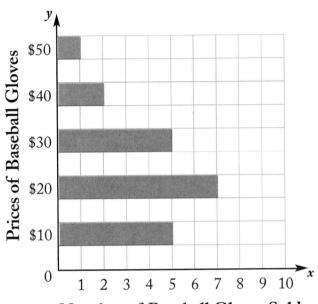

How many **$30** baseball gloves were sold?

Ⓐ   5 gloves

Ⓑ   7 gloves

Ⓒ 20 gloves

Ⓓ 30 gloves

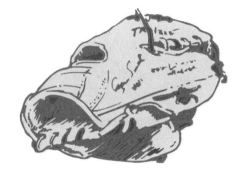

Go On

16. Jorge has a telescope that looks like this:

Which picture shows what the telescope would look like if it were turned 180°?

Ⓐ

Ⓒ

Ⓑ

Ⓓ

17. Lei An wants to know how hot it is outside. What instrument should she use?

Ⓐ protractor

Ⓑ ruler

Ⓒ scale

Ⓓ thermometer

Name ____________________ Class __________ Date __________

18. What number should go in the blank in order to make this number sentence true?

900 + _____ + 7 = 987

Ⓐ 8
Ⓑ 70
Ⓒ 80
Ⓓ 90

19. Mrs. Stafford is a teacher. In her bookcase, she has books about the subjects she teaches. If she picks one of the books without looking, which kind of book will she be **least** likely to pick?

Ⓐ history
Ⓑ mathematics
Ⓒ science
Ⓓ spelling

BOOKS ON SHELF	
Kind of Book	**Number**
History	28
Mathematics	4
Science	15
Spelling	2

20. Mr. Puso wants to put a fence around a play area for the preschool class. How many yards of fencing will he need for the play area below?

Ⓐ 18 yd

Ⓑ 20 yd

Ⓒ 22 yd

Ⓓ 23 yd

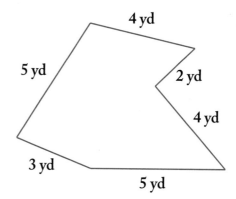

21. What number should go in the blank in order to make this number sentence true?

$(9 \times 3) - 4 = \underline{\quad} - 4$

Ⓐ 27

Ⓑ 24

Ⓒ 14

Ⓓ 12

22. On Monday, Jason bought a package that held small boxes of cereal. These are the cereal boxes in the package.

 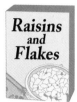  

He ate $\frac{3}{4}$ of the boxes of cereal during the week. How many boxes of cereal did he eat?

Ⓐ   3 boxes

Ⓑ   6 boxes

Ⓒ   9 boxes

Ⓓ 12 boxes

23. Which of these lengths is the **best estimate** for the length of a bed?

Ⓐ about 50 centimeters

Ⓑ about 2 meters

Ⓒ about 6 meters

Ⓓ about 1 kilometer

Go On

24. Esther made a square pyramid out of clay. How many **faces,** including the bottom, does the pyramid have?

ⓐ 3 faces

ⓑ 4 faces

ⓒ 5 faces

ⓓ 6 faces

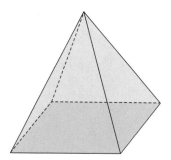

25. There are 4 green apples, 2 yellow apples, and 3 red apples in a bag. What are the chances of picking a **green apple** without looking?

ⓐ certain

ⓑ impossible

ⓒ most likely

ⓓ least likely

26. The perimeter of the figure below is 13 centimeters
(cm). What is the length of **side AB**?

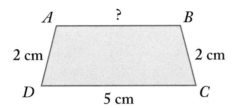

Ⓐ 2 cm

Ⓑ 4 cm

Ⓒ 6 cm

Ⓓ 8 cm

27. Pilar goes into a building that has an elevator. The
buttons in the elevator go from the ground floor
(floor 1) to the top floor (floor 7). About how tall is
the building?

Ⓐ about   70 feet tall

Ⓑ about   700 feet tall

Ⓒ about 1,400 feet tall

Ⓓ about 7,000 feet tall

**End of
Session 1**

Session 2

Directions: *There are 28 multiple-choice questions in this session. For each question, choose the best answer and mark your choice in the book.*

28. Find the missing factor that will make this number sentence true:

6 × _____ = 42

Ⓐ 4

Ⓑ 5

Ⓒ 6

Ⓓ 7

29. Which figure has **exactly one** circular face?

Ⓐ

Ⓒ

Ⓑ

Ⓓ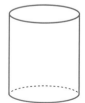

30. Which is the **best estimate** for the height of a door?

    Ⓐ 9 inches

    Ⓑ 7 feet

    Ⓒ 8 yards

    Ⓓ 3 miles

31. Soo Sung bought a ballpoint pen for 79¢. He gave the clerk a one-dollar bill. How much **change** did he get?

Ⓐ

Ⓑ

Ⓒ

Ⓓ

Go On

32. Which picture does NOT show the value one-half?

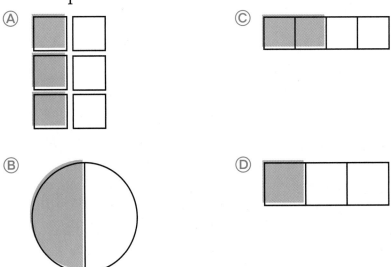

33. Barry left the house to go for a 2-hour bike ride. The clock below shows the time he left.

When did Barry get back?

Ⓐ   1 o'clock

Ⓑ   2 o'clock

Ⓒ   9 o'clock

Ⓓ   10 o'clock

34. Marisol has 20 marbles. Her two friends, Lena and Oriana, each have 9 marbles. Which answer shows the relationship between the number of marbles Marisol has and the numbers of marbles her friends have?

Ⓐ $20 > 9 + 9$

Ⓑ $20 < 9 + 9$

Ⓒ $20 = 9 + 9$

Ⓓ $20 + 9 < 9$

35. The James Monroe School had a book fair. The pictograph below shows the number of books ordered by each class. Which two grades ordered the **same number** of books?

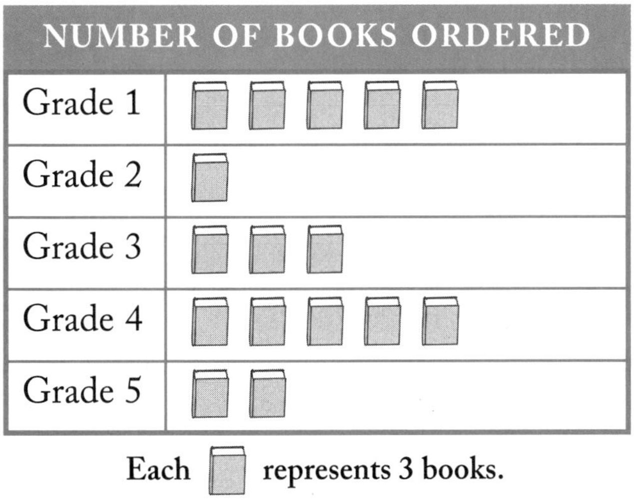

NUMBER OF BOOKS ORDERED	
Grade 1	▯ ▯ ▯ ▯ ▯
Grade 2	▯
Grade 3	▯ ▯ ▯
Grade 4	▯ ▯ ▯ ▯ ▯
Grade 5	▯ ▯

Each ▯ represents 3 books.

Ⓐ Grade 2 and Grade 4

Ⓑ Grade 3 and Grade 5

Ⓒ Grade 1 and Grade 2

Ⓓ Grade 1 and Grade 4

Go On

36. Mr. Gage wants to buy hot dogs for the family picnic. All the hot dog brands in the grocery store look the same. What units can Mr. Gage use to compare the different brands?

Ⓐ miles per hour

Ⓑ dollars per hour

Ⓒ miles per pound

Ⓓ dollars per pound

37. John, Iris, and Louise drove to Chicago. John drove 45 miles, and Iris drove 87 miles. Using this information, **which question** can you answer?

Ⓐ How long did it take to get to Chicago?

Ⓑ How much money did they spend on the trip?

Ⓒ How many more miles did Iris drive than John?

Ⓓ How many miles did Louise drive?

38. Keisha has drawn a picture of a flower.

Which of the following shows her picture after it has been flipped?

39. Karim has 106 shells in his collection. Maria has 95 shells. Juan has 188 shells. Using this information, which sentence is true?

Ⓐ Juan has about 100 shells.

Ⓑ Maria has about 100 more shells than Karim.

Ⓒ Juan has about half as many shells as Karim.

Ⓓ Together, Karim and Maria have about 200 shells.

Go On

40. Ruby is saving money to buy a pitcher's mitt. She is saving the same amount each week. Ruby expects to have enough money after **5 weeks.** How much does the mitt cost?

	1 Week	2 Weeks	3 Weeks	4 Weeks	5 Weeks
Total Saved	$6	$12	$18	?	?

Ⓐ $22

Ⓑ $24

Ⓒ $28

Ⓓ $30

41. Which figure is **congruent** to Figure 1?

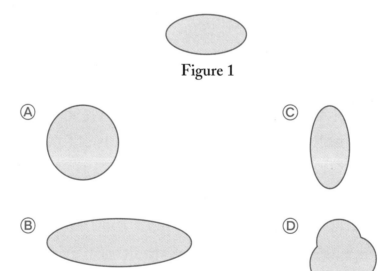

Figure 1

42. Mr. Kohn uses a column graph to keep track of the automobiles his salespeople sell each week. This week, they sold 8 sedans, 4 minivans, and 3 sport utility vehicles. Which graph shows this information?

(A) AUTOMOBILES SOLD

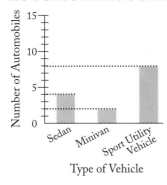

(C) AUTOMOBILES SOLD

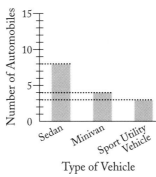

(B) AUTOMOBILES SOLD

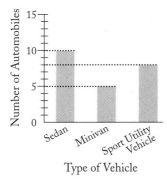

(D) AUTOMOBILES SOLD

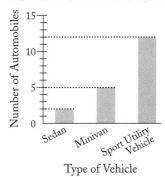

43. Between which two numbers does **468** go?

(A) between 40 and 49

(B) between 156 and 179

(C) between 201 and 329

(D) between 332 and 512

Go On

44. Look at the pattern below. Which pair of figures should go in the blanks in order to complete the pattern?

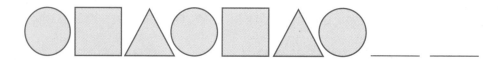

Ⓐ

Ⓒ

Ⓑ

Ⓓ

45. The blue line indicates one edge of the cube. How many **edges** does the cube have altogether?

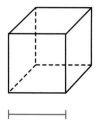

Ⓐ 4

Ⓑ 8

Ⓒ 10

Ⓓ 12

46. Marta made 10 paper dolls. She gave 3 dolls to each of her 3 friends. She had one doll left for herself. Which picture shows what Marta did?

Ⓐ

Ⓑ

Ⓒ

Ⓓ

47. Roberto has 24 blocks that he puts into stacks. Each stack has the same number of blocks in it. Which could NOT be the number of blocks in a stack?

Ⓐ 2 blocks

Ⓑ 3 blocks

Ⓒ 4 blocks

Ⓓ 5 blocks

Go On

48. A baseball team plans to buy some baseballs. Each baseball costs $3. If the team has $14, what is the **greatest** number of baseballs the players can buy?

Number of Baseballs	1	2	3	4	5	6
Cost	$3	$6	$9	$12	$15	$18

Ⓐ 3

Ⓑ 4

Ⓒ 5

Ⓓ 6

49. Look at the pattern below. Which way should the next letter P face in order to complete the pattern?

Ⓐ

Ⓒ

Ⓑ P

Ⓓ

50. What is the **area** of the figure below?

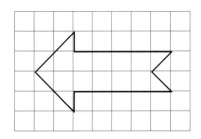

Ⓐ 10 square units

Ⓑ 12 square units

Ⓒ 13 square units

Ⓓ 16 square units

51. Look at the graph below. Which number pair represents the location of **point F**?

Ⓐ (3, 2)

Ⓑ (6, 4)

Ⓒ (2, 3)

Ⓓ (2, 2)

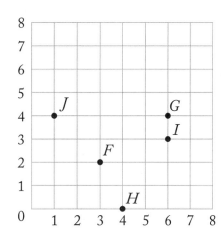

52. Which picture below shows the inequality
20 + 4 > 13 + 9?

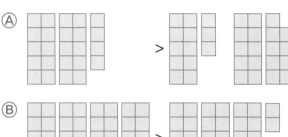

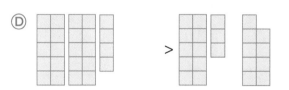

53. There are 12 colored pencils in a box. Three
pencils are red, 5 pencils are yellow, 2 pencils
are green, and 2 pencils are blue. Kevin
reaches into the box without looking
and takes a pencil. Which color is
Kevin **most likely** to get?

Ⓐ red

Ⓑ yellow

Ⓒ green

Ⓓ blue

54. Which number is the **biggest**?

Ⓐ 7,012

Ⓑ 4,999

Ⓒ 5,397

Ⓓ 7,020

55. Look at the fractions shown below. Which fraction is the **same** as $\frac{4}{10}$?

Ⓐ $\frac{1}{2}$

Ⓑ $\frac{2}{3}$

Ⓒ $\frac{2}{5}$

Ⓓ $\frac{3}{4}$

End of
Session 2

UNDERSTANDING THE FCAT MATH EXAM

Soon, you and other third graders in Florida will be taking a test called the FCAT. **FCAT** stands for Florida Comprehensive Assessment Test. This test will show how much you know about mathematics. Teachers from all over the state helped make a list of what you should know about math. Here are some of these goals:

- To know about numbers and how to work with them (how to add and multiply them, for example);

- To understand fractions;

- To know about measuring things and about making estimates;

- To know about number patterns and how to solve a number sentence;

- To know about flat shapes, like circles and squares, and about solid shapes, like spheres and cubes;

- To know how to make a graph or a chart;

- To know how to figure out the chance that something will happen.

The lessons in this book will help you to meet these goals. The exercises in each lesson will help you practice what you are learning. This will help you to do better work and be more ready to take the test.

What Is the FCAT Exam Like?

All the questions on the FCAT are multiple-choice. Each **multiple-choice question** gives you four possible answers. You should first solve the problem on scratch paper. Then choose the *best* answer choice and fill in the bubble next to that answer. Here is an example:

Katie's dog weighs 54 pounds. Mark's dog weighs 31 pounds. You want to know how much more Katie's dog weighs. Which number sentence should you use to find the answer?

Ⓐ 54 + 31 = ?

Ⓑ 31 + 54 = ?

Ⓒ 31 × 54 = ?

Ⓓ 54 − 31 = ?

In fourth grade, you will take another FCAT exam. It will be like the third-grade test. When you get to fifth grade, the FCAT will have different kinds of questions. Some of the questions are called **"Think, Solve, and Explain"** questions. They ask you to solve problems. You have to write each step of your math work. You have to say why you did it that way. This book will give you practice writing your own answers. Then you will be ready for the FCAT exams in the higher grades.

HOW TO USE THIS BOOK

I n the front of this book is a **Pretest** that you may have taken already. Don't worry if you missed some items! This book will help you to raise your score when you take the real test.

Lessons

The lessons in this **Introduction** will give you some helpful hints for taking all math tests, not just the FCAT. You will also learn about word problems. You will learn some words that give you clues for solving problems.

The lessons in Units 1–5 will teach you the skills you need to know to do well on any math exam. Each lesson in Units 1–5 follows the same pattern:

TITLE

- At the top is the **title** of the lesson, which tells you what the lesson is about.

The Challenge

- The first part of the lesson is called **The Challenge.** It gives you a hard problem to solve. This part has a picture of a mountain climber.

Learning the Ropes

- The next part is called **Learning the Ropes.** This will teach you the skills you need to know for this lesson.

Meeting the Challenge

- The next part is called **Meeting the Challenge.** This part shows you step by step how to solve the Challenge problem. There is another picture of a mountain climber here, but now the climber has reached the top of the mountain!

Each lesson also has other parts:

- **Math in History** tells you interesting facts from history that go with the lesson.

Math in History

- **Math in Use** tells how math skills are used in everyday life.

Math in Use

- **Another Way** shows you a new way to think about or solve the problems in the lesson. It has a picture of a person choosing between two different paths.

Try It Yourself

After each lesson, you will find two pages of math problems called **Try It Yourself.** First there are some multiple-choice questions, like the ones on the FCAT. Then there is a longer problem for extra practice. You have to write your own answer for each of these problems. At the end of the unit, there are more problems like that, for extra challenge.

Other Parts of the Book

Look for these other helpful parts of the book:

- The **Table of Contents** is at the front of this book. It tells you the page number where each lesson begins.

- The **Cumulative Review** gives you extra practice writing your own answers to problems.

- The **Posttest** is another test you can take, after you have done the lessons. If you have done the lessons, you will probably do much better on this test.

- The **Glossary** is at the back of this book. It can tell you what some of the important math words mean.

- The **Index** is at the very end of the book. It will tell you where each important idea is explained.

TIPS FOR TAKING THE FCAT MATH EXAM

It is normal to be nervous before any test. Almost everybody is at least a little nervous. By the time your class takes the FCAT exam, you will have learned a lot about math. If you prepare, you should be fine.

On the next three pages, you will find some tips to make the FCAT easier for you. Doing well on the state test is not the only reason to study this book, however. There are lots of math skills to learn in this book. They will help you to solve problems in your daily life.

During the Weeks Before the Test

✔ **Study.** It makes sense to study. The more you study, the more you will remember. Studying will make you feel better about taking the test. The better you feel, the better you will do!

✔ **Practice, practice, practice.** To be good at something, you must practice. To be a good skater, you must practice skating. To be good at math, you must practice math. One way is to do the "Try It Yourself" problems at the end of each lesson. Another way is to practice doing math in your head.

✔ **Use math every day.** Look at graphs and charts in newspapers and magazines. Notice amounts and measures in the kitchen and the stores. Look around you for math facts. There are math facts everywhere!

✔ **Review.** Once you have learned a lesson, go back later and look at it again. You will remember the lesson better if you do.

✔ **Take the Pretest and the Posttest.** Taking these practice tests will make taking the real test seem easier for you.

Just Before the Test

✔ **Gather the things you will need.** Ask your teacher what you need to bring. Make a list. The night before the test, put the things you will need together in one place. In the morning, they will be easy to find.

✔ **Get plenty of rest.** To do your best on the test, you need to be awake! Get plenty of sleep the night before the test. Your brain will work better if it is rested.

✔ **Eat a good breakfast.** Eating a good breakfast will give you energy. This will help you to stay alert while you are taking the test.

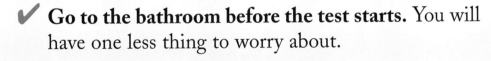

✔ **Go to the bathroom before the test starts.** You will have one less thing to worry about.

During the Test

✔ **Do your own work.** Do not cheat. It is wrong to cheat. It will not help you, and you will feel bad about yourself. You have studied and practiced. You don't need to look at other students' answers.

✔ **Follow directions.** Listen to what you are told to do. If you are not sure what to do, ask for help.

✔ **Read with care.** Read all the directions. Read the whole question before you try to answer it.

✔ **Look for clues.** Clues are hints about what you need to do. A word like *sum*, for example, is a clue that means you will need to add. If there is a picture or a graph, then look at it. Is there something in the picture that you already know? Have you seen a pattern like this somewhere else? How did you solve that problem?

✔ **Keep moving.** If a problem is too hard, skip it for now and come back to it later.

✔ **Find the best answer.** One good way to make it easier to choose is to get rid of answers you know are wrong.

✔ **Check your answer.** Does it make sense? Can you use an estimate to decide?

✔ **Make sure.** Did you fill in the right bubble? Did you erase any mistakes? Did you go back and answer any problems you skipped?

WORD PROBLEMS

Math exams usually have word problems. A **word problem** tells you about something that happens. It asks you to figure out something you do not know.

You use two kinds of math skills to solve word problems. The first math skill is reasoning. **Reasoning** helps you figure out what the problem is really about. The second math skill is solving. **Solving** a problem means doing the work to find an answer.

EXAMPLE Mr. Yu has two cows. If he buys two more cows, how many cows will he have?

This is a simple word problem. You probably already know the answer. First, you figured out that this problem is about adding. You might have thought, "I need to add two plus two." Once you used reasoning to figure out what the problem was, you could solve it. To solve the problem, you add two plus two and get four.

You use math every day. You figure out how long it is until recess. You figure out what temperature it is outside. You keep score in the games you play. You count your coins to see if you can buy something. The skills you use to solve everyday math are the same skills you can use for word problems.

How to Solve a Word Problem

1. **Figure out what you are being asked to find or do.** Read the whole problem. Look for clues. You will learn more about these clues in another lesson.

2. **Decide what the answer should look like.** Will the answer be a number? Will it be a picture? Do you need to find feet or yards? Do you need to find dollars and cents? Is more than one answer possible?

3. **Find the important facts.** What do you know? Write down what you know. Some problems on tests are messy. They give you lots of extra facts. Cross out the extra facts and use only the ones you need.

4. **Make a plan.** What strategy should you use to solve the problem? You will learn more about this in another lesson.

5. **Make an estimate.** Think about what the answer might be. Picture the numbers in your mind if you can.

6. **Check your answer.** One way to check your work is to see if your answer is close to your estimate. Another way to check is to see if your answer matches the facts in the problem.

Name _____ Class _____ Date _____

Try It Yourself

Fill in the circle next to the correct answer to each multiple-choice question.

1. Read this problem:

   The table below shows how many hot lunches the cafeteria sold on Monday and Friday for three different grades. About how many hot lunches were sold to students in all three grades on Friday?

HOT LUNCHES SOLD		
	Monday	**Friday**
Grade 3	74	119
Grade 4	56	134
Grade 5	28	99

   What are you being asked to find?

   Ⓐ the number of hot lunches sold on Monday

   Ⓑ an estimate of the hot lunches sold on Friday

   Ⓒ the exact number of third graders who bought hot lunches on Friday

   Ⓓ an estimate of the number of hot lunches sold on Monday and Friday

2. Read this problem:

   Hannah's vegetable garden is a triangle with sides that measure 35 yards, 22 yards, and 15 yards. When Hannah walks around her garden, how far does she walk?

   What should the answer look like?

   Ⓐ the number of yards

   Ⓑ the shape of the garden

   Ⓒ the time of year

   Ⓓ the kind of garden it is

3. Read this problem:

Patrick is adding stamps to his stamp album. He already has filled 16 pages in his album. If he adds 6 stamps in each of 4 rows on the next page, how many stamps does Patrick add to that page?

What are the important facts in this problem?

Ⓐ the number of stamps in each row and the number of rows

Ⓑ the total number of pages in the album

Ⓒ the number of pages in the album and the number of rows

Ⓓ the number of filled pages in the album

4. Read this problem:

Sandy brings 12 cookies to her scout meeting. If she runs out of cookies after she gives 2 cookies to each scout, how many scouts are at the meeting?

Which is the best plan to solve the problem?

Ⓐ Use addition.

Ⓑ Use subtraction.

Ⓒ Use multiplication.

Ⓓ Use division.

5. Read this problem:

Use your centimeter ruler to measure the length of the toothbrush shown. How many centimeters long is the toothbrush?

What might be a good estimate of the length?

Ⓐ 2 meters

Ⓑ 9 decimeters

Ⓒ 14 centimeters

Ⓓ 1 centimeter

STRATEGIES FOR SOLVING PROBLEMS

When you need to solve a problem, it helps to have a strategy. A **strategy** is a plan—a way to use the skills you know to find the answer. The best strategy is a plan that matches the problem. Using the right strategy makes solving the problem easier. Here are some good strategies that you can use.

STRATEGIES FOR MATH PROBLEMS

Act it out. When you use this strategy, you pretend to do what happens in the problem. Sometimes, it helps to use real objects. You may want to use chips or blocks to help.

Problem: Tracy has 15 stuffed animals. She puts 5 stuffed animals on each shelf. How many shelves does she use?

Strategy: Act it out. Use chips instead of stuffed animals. Lay out 15 chips in rows of 5. Each row will be one shelf. Count the rows.

Answer: Tracy uses 3 shelves.

Draw a picture. Your picture doesn't have to be perfect or beautiful. It just has to help you see what is going on. Label the parts.

Problem: Linda has two brothers and one sister. Linda's mom puts 3 cookies in each of her children's lunch bags. How many cookies does Linda's mom use?

Strategy: Draw a picture of four bags. Label each bag.

Draw 3 cookies in each bag. Count the cookies.

Answer: Linda's mom uses 12 cookies.

Make a table. This is a good strategy for keeping your facts in order. Decide what should go in each column of the table. Then figure out the rule that will explain what happens. Should you add? Subtract? Multiply? Divide?

Problem: Leah has been measuring her plant for science class. She kept a record of how tall the plant was each day for 5 days. The heights she measured were 3 centimeters, 5 centimeters, 6 centimeters, 9 centimeters, and 10 centimeters. The plant was 2 centimeters tall when Leah started keeping track of its height. On which day did the plant grow the most?

Strategy: Make a table. Give each day a number and write it in the first column. The second column will be the height measured. The third column will be the amount of growth for each day. The math rule that works is to subtract one height from the next.

Day	Height Measured	Amount Plant Grew
0	2 cm	—
1	3 cm	1 cm (because 3 – 2 = 1)
2	5 cm	2 cm (because 5 – 3 = 2)
3	6 cm	1 cm (because 6 – 5 = 1)
4	9 cm	3 cm (because 9 – 6 = 3)
5	10 cm	1 cm (because 10 – 9 = 1)

Answer: Leah's plant grew the most on Day 4. It grew 3 centimeters on that day.

Look for a pattern. Later in this book, you will learn more about patterns. In a pattern, the numbers can grow (get bigger), decrease (get smaller), or repeat themselves. Look to see what changes and what stays the same.

Problem: Ms. Fry has a bag of counting rods. She gives six rods to each child in her class. She counts out the rods in groups of six. The numbers go like this: 6, 12, 18, 24, …. What are the next three numbers?

Strategy: Look for a pattern. This is a growing pattern because the numbers keep getting bigger. What changes is the number of rods. The numbers go up by 6 each time.

Add 6 to 24 to get the first number.	$24 + 6 = 30$
Add 6 more to get the second number.	$30 + 6 = 36$
Add 6 more to get the third number.	$36 + 6 = 42$

Answer: The next three numbers are 30, 36, and 42.

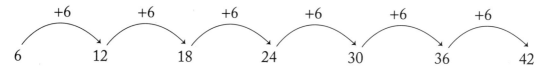

Guess and check. If you have a way to check, you can use this strategy. Try a possible answer. See if your answer is too high or too low. Try again with a better guess. For multiple-choice questions, use only the choices given. Try each choice until you find the one that works.

Problem: Toby finds two coins in the sofa. He finds 35¢. What are the two coins?

Strategy: Guess and check. The two coins must add up to 35¢.

Guess 5¢ and 5¢, and check.	$5¢ + 5¢ = 10¢.$	*Too low.*
Guess 25¢ and 25¢, and check.	$25¢ + 25¢ = 50¢.$	*Too high.*
Guess 10¢ and 10¢, and check.	$10¢ + 10¢ = 20¢.$	*Too low.*
Guess 10¢ and 25¢, and check.	$25¢ + 10¢ = 35¢.$	*Correct.*

Answer: The two coins Toby finds are a quarter and a dime.

Work backward. Start with what you know at the end of the problem. Work back to the start to solve the problem.

Problem: Johan has 2 fewer fish than Andy does. Andy has 6 more fish than Raj. Raj has 3 fish. How many fish does Johan have?

Strategy: Work backward. Start with what you know at the end.

Raj has 3 fish.

Work back from that. You know that Andy has 6 more fish than Raj.

> Add 6 to 3:
> 6 + 3 = 9

Andy has 9 fish.

Keep working back. You know that Johan has 2 fewer fish than Andy.

> Subtract 2 from 9:
> 9 − 2 = 7

Answer: Johan has 7 fish.

Work a simpler problem. Change messy or complicated numbers to numbers that are easier to work with. Solve the simpler problem. Then use the way you solved the simpler problem to help solve the harder problem.

Problem: Between what two numbers would 325 appear? Choose one of the answers below.

Ⓐ 140 and 275

Ⓑ 270 and 436

Ⓒ 420 and 526

Ⓓ 524 and 626

Strategy: Work a simpler problem. Change the messy numbers to simpler numbers.

Simpler problem: Between what two numbers would 3 appear? (Make it easy: Use 3 instead of 325.)

Ⓐ 1 and 2 (Use 1 and 2 instead of 140 and 275.)

Ⓑ 2 and 4 (Use 2 and 4 instead of 270 and 436.)

Ⓒ 4 and 5 (Use 4 and 5 instead of 420 and 526.)

Ⓓ 5 and 6 (Use 5 and 6 instead of 524 and 626.)

Answer: Ⓑ 270 and 436. (The number 325 is between these two, just as the number 3 is between 2 and 4.)

Try It Yourself

Fill in the circle next to the correct answer to each multiple-choice question.

1. Dana started with 57 baseball cards. Her brother gave her 36 of his cards. Dana traded 12 of her cards for 8 of Ali's cards. Which problem-solving strategy would help you to find how many cards Dana had after she traded with Ali?

    Ⓐ guess and check   Ⓒ look for a pattern

    Ⓑ use a simpler problem   Ⓓ act it out

2. Read this problem:

    Mike is stocking shelves at the bookstore. Each time he makes a trip to the storeroom, he brings back 5 books. Mike makes 3 trips to the storeroom. How many books does he carry in all?

    Which of the following drawings shows how to solve this problem?

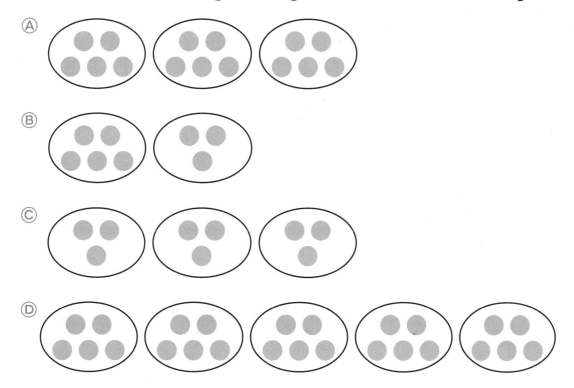

Go On →

3. Look at this pattern of numbers.

    7   14   21   28   35   ____   ____   ____

    What is the eighth number in this pattern?

    Ⓐ 42   Ⓑ 56   Ⓒ 63   Ⓓ 81

4. Gina has 8 coins in her piggy bank. She puts only dimes and nickels in the bank. She has 70¢ in her bank. How many dimes does she have? Use a guess-and-check strategy.

    Ⓐ 3   Ⓑ 4   Ⓒ 5   Ⓓ 6

5. Jess earns $8 each time that she mows the lawn. Which of the following tables would you use to find how much money Jess earns if she mows the lawn 4 times?

Ⓐ

Mowing	$ Earned
1 time	$ 8
2 times	$10
3 times	$13
4 times	$17

Ⓒ

Mowing	$ Earned
1 time	$ 8
2 times	$16
3 times	$24
4 times	$32

Ⓑ

Mowing	$ Earned
1 time	$ 8
2 times	$12
3 times	$16
4 times	$20

Ⓓ

Mowing	$ Earned
1 time	$ 8
2 times	$ 9
3 times	$10
4 times	$11

WORDS WITH SPECIAL MATH MEANINGS

What should you do when you read a word problem? The first thing to do is to read with care. As you read the problem, look for words that have special math meanings. This book will teach you many new words that will help you solve problems. These words are in **bold** letters. The meaning of each new math word is explained the first time the word appears. If you are not sure what a math word means, you can also look it up in the Glossary at the back of this book.

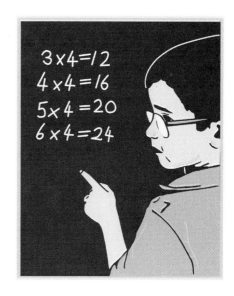

Besides the math words, look for common words that give you hints about what to do. Words such as *more* and *in all* help you figure out when to add, subtract, multiply, or divide. The charts on the next four pages show some words that give you clues about what to do in a problem.

Addition. Addition is the joining together of two or more groups. Here are some words that often mean you should use addition:

Words That Go with Addition	Examples
and	How long is a 2-foot kite **and** a 10-foot tail? ADD: 2 + 10
combine	Max **combined** his 14 cards with Tara's 8 cards. ADD: 14 + 8
in all	I have 3 chips, Donny has 2 chips, and Sara has 1 chip. How many chips do we have **in all**? ADD: 3 + 2 + 1
more	Rose has 2 **more** kittens than Yvette. Yvette has 3 kittens. How many kittens does Rose have? ADD: 3 + 2
sum	Find the **sum** of 5, 7, and 12. ADD: 5 + 7 + 12
total	The two booths at the school fair made $6 and $5. How much did they make in **total**? ADD: 6 + 5

Subtraction. When you subtract, you take away some things from a group. Here are some words that usually mean you should use subtraction:

Words That Go with Subtraction	Examples
fewer	Madeline made 13 valentines. Her friend Alison made 3 **fewer** valentines. How many valentines did Alison make? SUBTRACT: 13 – 3
left, left over	There are 9 centimeters of ribbon on the table. Mary Beth cuts off 2 centimeters. How much ribbon is **left**? SUBTRACT: 9 – 2
how many more	Kit has 7 marbles. Marti has 9 marbles. **How many more** marbles does Marti have? SUBTRACT: 9 – 7
take away	Seven puppies are in a box. If you **take away** 3 puppies, how many are left? SUBTRACT: 7 – 3
remain	If Marla spends 12 of her 15 pennies, how many pennies will **remain**? SUBTRACT: 15 – 12

The words you have just learned can help you solve a problem. However, the most important thing is to read the whole problem with care. For example, the word **more** can mean to add, but the words **how many more** mean to subtract.

Multiplication. Both multiplication and addition mean finding a total amount. Multiplication uses equal groups. Here are some clue words for multiplication:

Words That Go with Multiplication	Examples
double	Kalil invited 3 friends for a sleepover. Cara had **double** that number of friends for her sleepover. How many friends did Cara have at her sleepover? MULTIPLY: 3×2
triple	One scoop of ice cream weighs 4 ounces. Michael had a **triple** scoop. How much did it weigh? MULTIPLY: 4×3
product	Find the **product** of 5 and 6. MULTIPLY: 5×6
times	How much is 2 **times** 8? MULTIPLY: 2×8
twice	There are 4 people in Doug's family. There are **twice** as many people in David's family. How many people are in David's family? MULTIPLY: 4×2

Division. When you divide, you may be trying to find the number of equal parts in a whole. You also divide to find the size of the equal parts. Division is used when people want to share things equally. Here are some division clues:

Words That Go with Division	Examples
half	Cherise had 6 cookies. She gave **half** to Dionne. How many cookies did Dionne get? DIVIDE: $6 \div 2$
third	Miguel and his two cousins had 12 oranges. Miguel got a **third** of the oranges. How many oranges did Miguel get? DIVIDE: $12 \div 3$
shared equally	Raymond and Skyler had 14 baseball cards. If they **shared equally,** how many baseball cards did Skyler get? DIVIDE: $14 \div 2$
split, split up	The scout leader **split up** the 12 campers into 4 tents. How many campers were in each tent? DIVIDE: $12 \div 4$

Test-Taking Words. When you take a test, there are some important words that you should look for. These special test-taking words will tell what kind of answer to look for.

Test-Taking Words	Examples
not	Samantha has more grapes than Eileen. Eileen has 5 grapes. Which answer is **not** a number of grapes that Samantha could have? 4, 6, 8, or 10? FIND THE ONLY WRONG ANSWER: 4 is not more than 5.
pattern, rule	Gerald got 2 postcards on Monday. On Tuesday, he got 5 postcards. On Wednesday, he got 8 postcards. If the **pattern** continues, how many postcards will Gerald get on Thursday? FIRST FIND THE PATTERN. THEN FIND THE ANSWER: The rule is "add 3 each day." Gerald will get $8 + 3 = 11$.
most, largest	Danny has 312 pennies, Sammy has 213 pennies, Scott has 132 pennies, and Nora has 231 pennies. Who has the **most**? FIND THE LARGEST NUMBER: 312 is the largest.
least, smallest	Who has the **least** number of pennies? FIND THE SMALLEST NUMBER: 132 is the smallest.
estimate, about	Vince and Rhonda are stacking chairs. Vince has stacked 197 chairs. Rhonda has stacked 98 chairs. **Estimate** the number of chairs they have stacked together. USE EASIER NUMBERS THAT ARE ABOUT THE SAME: 197 is about 200, and 98 is about 100. $200 + 100 =$ about 300

Name _____ Class _____ Date _____

Try It Yourself

Fill in the circle next to the correct answer to each multiple-choice question.

1. Read this problem:

   Daisy wrote a story that was 6 pages long. Ed's story had 3 pages more than Daisy's story. How many pages long was Ed's story?

   Which of these number statements would you use to solve this problem?

   Ⓐ 6 + 3 　　　Ⓑ 6 × 3 　　　Ⓒ 6 − 3 　　　Ⓓ 6 ÷ 3

2. Sal has 16 toy cars and 8 toy trucks.

   Which of these questions can be answered using subtraction?

   Ⓐ How many fewer toy trucks than toy cars does Sal have?

   Ⓑ If he splits his toy cars into groups of 4, how many cars will be in each group?

   Ⓒ If he combines his toy cars and toy trucks, how many toys will he have in all?

   Ⓓ Does he have twice as many toy cars as trucks?

3. Read this problem:

   Tom knows 9 magic tricks. His granddad teaches him 3 more. How many tricks does Tom know in all?

   Which of these number statements would you use to solve this problem?

   Ⓐ 9 + 3 　　　Ⓑ 9 − 3 　　　Ⓒ 9 × 3 　　　Ⓓ 9 ÷ 3

4. Read this problem:

   Sonya has 4 aunts and 2 uncles. How many more aunts than uncles does Sonya have?

   Which of these number statements would you use to solve this problem?

   Ⓐ 4 + 2 　　　Ⓑ 4 − 2 　　　Ⓒ 4 × 2 　　　Ⓓ 4 ÷ 2

Go On

5. Read this problem:

   Sara passed out 3 sheets of paper to each of the 6 children in her group. How many sheets of paper did Sara pass out?

   Which of these number statements would you use to solve this problem?

   Ⓐ 3 + 6   Ⓑ 3 × 6   Ⓒ 6 − 3   Ⓓ 6 ÷ 3

6. Read this problem:

   Kent and Carol have $18. They split up the money equally into 2 envelopes. How much money is in each envelope?

   Which of these number statements would you use to solve this problem?

   Ⓐ 18 + 2   Ⓑ 18 × 2   Ⓒ 18 − 2   Ⓓ 18 ÷ 2

7. Read this problem:

   Wes earned $8 on Friday and half that amount on Saturday. How much money did Wes earn on Saturday?

   Which of these number statements would you use to solve this problem?

   Ⓐ $8 + 2   Ⓑ $8 × 2   Ⓒ $8 − 2   Ⓓ $8 ÷ 2

8. Fred and Pat practiced throwing a football. Pat threw the football 9 yards.

   Which of these questions can best be answered using multiplication?

   Ⓐ If Fred threw the football 12 yards, how much farther was Fred's throw than Pat's?

   Ⓑ If Fred threw the football 3 yards farther than Pat did, how far was Fred's throw?

   Ⓒ If Fred threw the football a third as far as Pat did, how far was Fred's throw?

   Ⓓ Fred threw the football twice as far as Pat did. How far was Fred's throw?

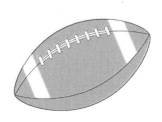

PLACE VALUE

This lesson addresses Benchmarks MA.A.1.2.1, MA.A.1.2.3, MA.A.1.2.4, and MA.A.2.2.1 of the Sunshine State Standards.

Math in History
Every ten years since 1790, the U.S. Government has counted the number of people living in this country. This count is called the **census.** Some towns have only a few hundred people. Some cities have thousands of people. Big cities have millions of people! How many people live in your town or city?

The Challenge

Michael's school collects cans for recycling. Last year, students collected 96,325 cans. This year, students hope to collect one hundred twenty thousand cans.

Write 96,325 in word form. Write the standard form of one hundred twenty thousand.

Learning the Ropes

Every number is made up of **digits.** Each of the numbers from zero to nine (0, 1, 2, 3, 4, 5, 6, 7, 8, and 9) is a digit. The number 10 has two digits, 1 and 0. The **value** of each digit, or how much it is worth, depends upon its place in the number.

A **place-value chart** shows the value of each digit in a number. Each group of three digits in a whole number is called a **period.** This place-value chart shows the thousands period and the ones period.

Thousands Period			Ones Period		
hundreds	tens	ones	hundreds	tens	ones
	3	4,	9	0	2

The 9 in this number is worth nine hundred (900) because it is in the hundreds place. The 3 in this number is worth thirty thousand (30,000) because it is in the ten-thousands place.

Unit 1: Number Sense, Concepts, and Operations

Math in Use: Water Conservation A big freshwater spring (a first-magnitude spring) can produce more than eight million, six hundred forty thousand cubic feet of water per day. Florida has more first-magnitude springs than almost any other state. Altogether, Florida's springs produce over eight billion gallons of water per day. These numbers are written in standard form as 8,640,000 and 8,000,000,000.

You can write the number shown in the chart on the previous page in different forms.

Standard Form: 34,902

Word Name: thirty-four thousand, nine hundred two

The place-value chart on the previous page shows that the number has 3 ten thousands and 4 thousands, so we read the first part as "thirty-four thousand." The chart also shows that the number has 9 hundreds and 2 ones, but it does not have any tens. We read the last part (period) as "nine hundred two."

Meeting the Challenge

To answer the Challenge, you must write the word name of one number and the standard form of another number.

STEP 1: Write the word form of 96,325 as you would read it. Remember to write commas between periods.

Standard Form	Word Name
96,325	ninety-six thousand, three hundred twenty-five

STEP 2: Write the standard form of one hundred twenty thousand. Write the 3-digit number for the thousands period first (120). Then write zeros for the ones, tens, and hundreds in this number.

Word Name	Standard Form
one hundred twenty thousand	120,000

Another Way If you are having trouble reading a large number, try writing it in a place-value chart.

Thousands Period			Ones Period		
hundreds	tens	ones	hundreds	tens	ones
	9	6,	3	2	5

Name _____ Class _____ Date _____

Try It Yourself

A. Fill in the circle next to the correct answer to each multiple-choice question.

1. What is the value of the 8 in 38,061?
   Ⓐ 80,000   Ⓑ 8,000   Ⓒ 80   Ⓓ 8

2. Which answer is the same number as 240,307?
   Ⓐ twenty-four thousand, thirty-seven
   Ⓑ twenty-four thousand, three hundred seven
   Ⓒ two hundred forty, three hundred seven thousand
   Ⓓ two hundred forty thousand, three hundred seven

3. Which answer shows ninety-seven thousand, six hundred in standard form?
   Ⓐ 9,700,600   Ⓑ 970,600   Ⓒ 97,600   Ⓓ 976

4. The number of people living in Florida in the year 2000 was 15,952,000. What is the word name for this number?
   Ⓐ fifteen billion, nine hundred fifty-two million
   Ⓑ fifteen billion, nine hundred fifty-two thousand
   Ⓒ fifteen million, nine hundred fifty-two thousand
   Ⓓ fifteen million, nine hundred fifty-two

5. Sound travels sixty-five thousand, two hundred eighty feet in one minute. What is the standard form for this number?
   Ⓐ 65,200,80   Ⓑ 65,280   Ⓒ 65,208   Ⓓ 65,028

6. The average human adult heart beats one hundred three thousand, six hundred eighty times in one day. What is the standard form of this number?
   Ⓐ 13,680   Ⓒ 136,080
   Ⓑ 130,608   Ⓓ 103,680

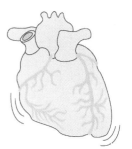

Go On ➤

7. The tallest mountain in the United States is Mt. McKinley (Denali). It is 20,320 feet high. What is the word name of this number?

   Ⓐ twenty thousand, three hundred twenty

   Ⓑ two thousand, thirty-two

   Ⓒ twenty, three hundred twenty thousand

   Ⓓ two thousand, three hundred twenty

8. The Ryders want to buy a car that is priced at $23,950. The salesperson will sell it for one thousand dollars less. What is the new price of the car?

   Ⓐ $13,950   Ⓑ $22,950   Ⓒ $23,850   Ⓓ $24,950

B. Complete the two parts below. Show all your work.

Use the place-value models below to answer Parts A and B.

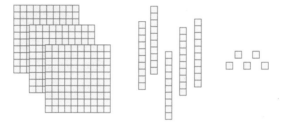

Part A What number is shown by the place-value models? Explain your answer. (Each big square stands for 100.)

Part B If you took away one big square and one little square from the drawing above, what new number would be shown? Write a number sentence to show this problem.

COMPARING AND ORDERING NUMBERS

This lesson addresses Benchmark MA.A.1.2.2 of the Sunshine State Standards.

Math in History
Did you know that dinosaurs varied greatly in size? *Iguanodon* weighed about 9,900 pounds. Another dinosaur, *Oviraptor,* weighed about 45 pounds. *Troodon* weighed about 110 pounds. *Compsognathus* weighed only about 7 pounds. Can you put these weights in order from least to greatest?

The Challenge

Kellie lives in Jacksonville, Florida. The table shows the driving distances between her city and three other cities. Write the cities in order by distance from Jacksonville (from greatest to least).

DISTANCE FROM JACKSONVILLE	
City	**Distance (miles)**
Denver, CO	1,750
New York, NY	945
Chicago, IL	1,064

Learning the Ropes

When you **compare** numbers, you see which one is bigger and which one is smaller. The **inequality** symbol > means "is greater than." The symbol < means "is less than." The fat (open) side of the symbol is always toward the bigger number. The skinny (closed) side points to the smaller number.

You can use place value to help compare **whole numbers** (0, 1, 2, 3, etc.) and put them in order. Write the numbers in a place-value chart or in columns. Make sure that you line up the ones digits. Starting at the left, compare the digits in each column until you find a column that has different digits. Then compare those digits.

EXAMPLE Order 817; 4,526; and 4,503 from least to greatest. Put the numbers into a place-value chart.

Thousands			Ones		
hundreds	**tens**	**ones**	**hundreds**	**tens**	**ones**
			8	1	7
		4,	5	2	6
		4,	5	0	3

Unit 1: Number Sense, Concepts, and Operations   **63**

You know that 817 is less than the other two numbers because it does not have any thousands. To compare 4,526 and 4,503, start from the left. Both numbers have a 4 in the thousands place and a 5 in the hundreds place. The number 4,526 has 2 tens, and 4,503 has zero tens. Because 0 tens is less than 2 tens, 4,503 < 4,526. Now, you are ready to write all three numbers in order:

$$817 < 4,503 < 4,526$$

Meeting the Challenge

To answer the Challenge, you need to put the distances from Jacksonville to the other cities in order from greatest to least.

> 1,750
> 945
> 1,064

STEP 1: Write the numbers of miles in a place-value chart or in columns. Remember to line up the ones digits.

STEP 2: Check to see if any one number has more or fewer digits than the others. The number 945 has the fewest digits. It is the least number of miles.

STEP 3: Compare the other numbers. Both have 1 in the thousands place. The number 1,750 has 7 hundreds, and 1,064 has no hundreds. Thus, 1,750 > 1,064.

STEP 4: Write the numbers in order from greatest to least.

Numbers:　　　　　*Cities:*
1,750 > 1,064 > 945　　Denver, Chicago, New York

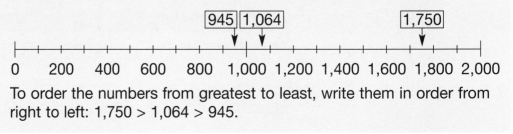

Another Way You can also use a number line to order numbers. The numbers on a number line get bigger as you move from left to right.

EXAMPLE Order these three numbers from greatest to least.

To order the numbers from greatest to least, write them in order from right to left: 1,750 > 1,064 > 945.

Name _____ Class _____ Date _____

Try It Yourself

A. Fill in the circle next to the correct answer to each multiple-choice question.

1. Which number sentence is true?
   Ⓐ 7,004 > 7,010 Ⓑ 4,105 < 853 Ⓒ 5,006 < 605 Ⓓ 3,254 > 3,217

2. The Nuñez family is planning to buy a computer. Which of these prices is the least amount of money?
   Ⓐ $1,770 Ⓑ $1,749 Ⓒ $1,829 Ⓓ $1,800

3. The school librarian keeps track of all the different books that third graders check out. The table shows the number of books that each of the four classes read this year.

BOOKS THIRD GRADERS READ	
Class	**Number of Books**
A	116
B	96
C	112
D	106

   Which statement is true?
   Ⓐ Class A read more books than Class C.
   Ⓑ Class B read more books than Class C.
   Ⓒ Class C read fewer books than Class D.
   Ⓓ Class D read fewer books than Class B.

4. Toya has four number cards: 5, 7, 8, 3. What is the smallest number she can make using all the cards?
   Ⓐ 3,587 Ⓑ 3,785 Ⓒ 3,578 Ⓓ 3,758

5. The table shows when four important events in the history of the United States happened. Which list shows these dates in order from earliest to most recent?

Ⓐ 1962, 1865, 1845, 1789
Ⓑ 1789, 1845, 1865, 1962
Ⓒ 1962, 1845, 1865, 1789
Ⓓ 1789, 1845, 1962, 1865

Event in U.S. History	Year
First American in space orbits Earth	1962
Civil War ends	1865
Florida becomes a state	1845
Washington elected president	1789

6. Which number sentence below is represented by these models?

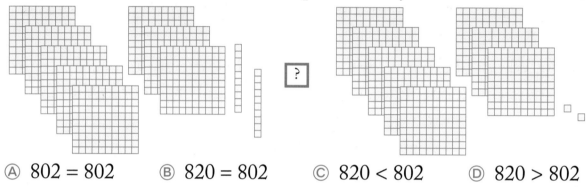

Ⓐ 802 = 802   Ⓑ 820 = 802   Ⓒ 820 < 802   Ⓓ 820 > 802

B. Complete the activity below.

The table shows the lengths of four rivers in the United States. Write the names of these four rivers in order from longest to shortest.

U.S. RIVERS	
River	**Length (miles)**
Missouri	2,540
Rio Grande	1,900
Mississippi	2,302
Red	1,290

THE MEANING OF ADDITION AND SUBTRACTION

This lesson addresses Benchmarks MA.A.3.2.1 and MA.A.3.2.2 of the Sunshine State Standards.

Math in History

About 4,500 years ago, the ancient Egyptians began the construction of the pyramids of Giza. For many years, it was thought that the number of stones in the 450-foot-tall Great Pyramid of Khufu was more than 2 million. A more accurate count was done in 2002. The estimated number of stones used dropped to just 1 million. Using subtraction, you can see that the first count was wrong by more than 1 million stones!

The Challenge

Kim had 8 fish in her aquarium. On Saturday, she gave 2 fish to a friend. On Monday, she bought 3 more fish. How many fish did Kim have on Monday?

Learning the Ropes

You can use **addition** to find the total number when two or more groups of items are joined together.

EXAMPLE

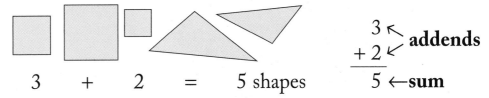

$$3 \quad + \quad 2 \quad = \quad 5 \text{ shapes}$$

$$\begin{array}{r} 3 \\ + 2 \\ \hline 5 \end{array} \leftarrow \text{addends} \\ \leftarrow \textbf{sum}$$

Ways that numbers behave are called **properties.** The **commutative property of addition** says that changing the order of the addends does not change the sum.

EXAMPLE $\quad 2 + 5 = 7$ is the same as $5 + 2 = 7$.

The **associative property of addition** says that changing the way addends are grouped does not change the sum.

EXAMPLE $\quad (3 + 4) + 2 = 9$ and $3 + (4 + 2) = 9$.
$\quad\quad\quad\quad\quad 7 \quad + 2 = 9$ and $3 + \quad 6 \quad = 9$.

The **identity property for addition** says that any number plus zero equals that number.

EXAMPLE $\quad 4 + 0 = 4$ and $0 + 4 = 4$.

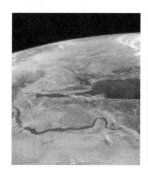

You can use **subtraction** to find how many are left when a number of items are taken away from a group. You can also use subtraction to find the difference when two groups of items are compared.

EXAMPLE

6   −   4   = 2 more squares

$$6 \leftarrow \textbf{minuend}$$
$$\underline{- 4} \leftarrow \textbf{subtrahend}$$
$$2 \leftarrow \textbf{difference}$$

Addition and subtraction are opposites of each other. A **fact family** contains the addition and subtraction facts that use the same numbers.

EXAMPLES

| $3 + 4 = 7$ $7 - 4 = 3$ |
| $4 + 3 = 7$ $7 - 3 = 4$ |

| $5 + 5 = 10$ $10 - 5 = 5$ |

Meeting the Challenge

To answer the Challenge, you must find the number of fish Kim had after she gave some away and then bought some more.

STEP 1: Use subtraction to find how many fish Kim had left.

$8 - 2 = 6$ fish   Kim had 6 fish left on Saturday.

STEP 2: Use addition to find how many fish Kim had after buying some more.

$6 + 3 = 9$ fish   Kim had 9 fish on Monday.

Kim had 9 fish after giving 2 away and then buying 3 more.

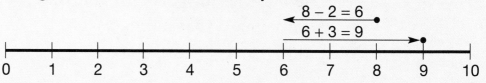

Another Way You can also use a number line to add and subtract. Go right to add, and move left when you subtract.

$8 - 2 = 6$
$6 + 3 = 9$

0 1 2 3 4 5 6 7 8 9 10

Try It Yourself

A. Fill in the circle next to the correct answer to each multiple-choice question.

1. Carla has 8 animal stickers and 3 flower stickers. How many more animal stickers than flower stickers does she have?

   Ⓐ 4   Ⓑ 5   Ⓒ 8   Ⓓ 11

2. Which statement is true?

   Ⓐ When you add zero to any number, the sum is that number.

   Ⓑ When you subtract zero from a number, the difference is zero.

   Ⓒ When you add zero to any number, the sum is zero.

   Ⓓ When you subtract any number from itself, the difference is that number.

3. Which shows the complete fact family that uses the numbers 6, 7, and 13?

   Ⓐ $6 + 7 = 13$
                         Ⓒ $6 + 7 = 13$

       $7 + 6 = 13$
                            $7 + 6 = 13$

       $6 + 13 = 19$
                       Ⓓ $6 + 7 = 13$

       $7 + 13 = 20$
                            $7 + 6 = 13$

   Ⓑ $6 + 7 = 13$
                           $13 - 6 = 7$

       $13 - 7 = 6$
                            $13 - 7 = 6$

4. Which number will make this sentence true?

   $$5 + (3 + 2) = (5 + \underline{}) + 2$$

   Ⓐ 2   Ⓑ 3   Ⓒ 5   Ⓓ 10

5. Which number sentence is true?

   Ⓐ $7 - 7 = 7$
                       Ⓒ $9 - 7 = 7 - 9$

   Ⓑ $8 - 0 = 8$
                       Ⓓ $(10 - 6) - 2 = 10 - (6 - 2)$

Go On

6. Suppose that you found the sum of 752 and 88. Which number sentence does NOT show a way that you could check your answer?

Ⓐ $88 + 752 = \Box$ Ⓒ $752 - 88 = \Box$

Ⓑ $\Box - 88 = 752$ Ⓓ $\Box - 752 = 88$

7. Ricardo is 9 years old. His little sister is 4. Which problem tells how old Ricardo was when his sister was born?

Ⓐ $9 + 4$ Ⓑ $4 + 9$ Ⓒ $9 - 4$ Ⓓ $4 - 9$

8. Complete the three parts below. Show all your work.

The table below shows how many pets Sam has. Use the table to answer Parts A–C.

SAM'S PETS	
Pet	**Number**
Fish	9
Dogs	3
Gerbils	5
Birds	2

Part A Write a number sentence to show how many birds and fish Sam has.

Part B Write a number sentence to show how many more fish than gerbils Sam has.

Part C Write a number sentence to show how many pets Sam has that do not live in water.

ADDING WHOLE NUMBERS

This lesson addresses Benchmarks MA.A.3.2.2 and MA.A.3.2.3 of the Sunshine State Standards.

The Challenge

The third graders at Valley Elementary School put on a play. The table shows the number of tickets they sold for Saturday afternoon. How many tickets were sold in all for Saturday afternoon?

Type of Ticket	Number of Tickets
Seniors	97
Adults	206
Children	353

Math in History
Some animals, like dinosaurs, became **extinct** (disappeared from the Earth) a long time ago. Animals that are now in danger of becoming extinct are called **endangered** or **threatened.** About 342 mammals, 273 birds, 126 fish, and 115 reptiles world-wide are endangered or threatened. Altogether, how many mammals and birds are endangered or threatened? How many fish and reptiles? What other questions could you answer by adding these numbers?

Learning the Ropes

When you add numbers with two or three digits, first write them in a column. Be sure to line up the ones digits. Start at the right and add the ones, then the tens, and then the hundreds. You might need to **regroup.** For example, if the ones column adds up to 10 or more, change 10 ones into 1 ten.

EXAMPLE   Add 716 and 829.

STEP 1:
Add the ones:
  6 + 9 = 15
Regroup:
  15 ones = 1 ten + 5 ones

Extra one from regrouping in Step 1

STEP 2:
Add the tens:
  1 + 1 + 2 = 4
Regrouping is
  not necessary.

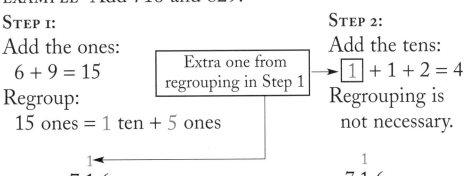

$$\begin{array}{r} 1 \\ 7\,1\,6 \\ +8\,2\,9 \\ \hline 5 \end{array}$$

$$\begin{array}{r} 1 \\ 7\,1\,6 \\ +8\,2\,9 \\ \hline 4\,5 \end{array}$$

Steps continued on next page

Math in Use: Agriculture In the 1999–2000 growing season, Florida produced about 134 million boxes of navel oranges, 99 million boxes of Valencia oranges, and 53 million, 400 thousand boxes of grapefruit. Did Florida produce more boxes of Valencia oranges and grapefruit than boxes of navel oranges? What addition problem would you do to find out?

STEP 3:
Add the hundreds:
7 + 8 = 15
Regroup: 15 hundreds
 = 1 thousand + 5 hundreds

```
   1   1
     7 1 6
   +8 2 9
   ───────
   1,5 4 5
```

STEP 4:
Check by changing the
 order of the addends
 and adding again:

```
   1   1
     8 2 9
   +7 1 6
   ───────
   1,5 4 5
```

Meeting the Challenge

To answer the Challenge, you need to write the three numbers in a column and add them to find how many tickets were sold in all.

STEP 1:
Add the ones:
7 + 6 + 3 = 16
Regroup: 16 ones =
 1 ten + 6 ones

```
       1
      9 7
      2 0 6
    +3 5 3
    ───────
          6
```

STEP 2:
Add the tens:
1 + 9 + 0 + 5 = 15
Regroup: 15 tens =
 1 hundred + 5 tens

```
     1 1
      9 7
      2 0 6
    +3 5 3
    ───────
        5 6
```

STEP 3:
Add the hundreds:
1 + 2 + 3 = 6
Regrouping is
 not necessary.

```
     1 1
      9 7
      2 0 6
    +3 5 3
    ───────
      6 5 6
```

STEP 4:
Check by adding in
 a different order:

```
     1 1
      3 5 3
      2 0 6
    +   9 7
    ───────
      6 5 6
```

A total of 656 tickets were sold for the Saturday afternoon performance.

Another Way To keep your columns lined up, you might find it helpful to write the numbers that you are adding on lined paper turned sideways. Remember, you can write only one digit from each number in each column.

	1	1		○
		9	7	
	2	0	6	
+	3	5	3	
	6	5	6	

Name _____ Class _____ Date _____

Try It Yourself

A. Fill in the circle next to the correct answer to each multiple-choice question.

1. What is the sum of the numbers represented by these place-value models?

Ⓐ 514   Ⓑ 64   Ⓒ 54   Ⓓ 19

2. There are 852 cars, 23 buses, and 395 trucks in a parking lot. How many vehicles are there in all?

   Ⓐ 1,160 vehicles

   Ⓑ 1,260 vehicles

   Ⓒ 1,270 vehicles

   Ⓓ 1,279 vehicles

3. Sara worked the four problems shown below for homework. She worked only one problem correctly. Which problem did Sara work correctly?

   Ⓐ
   $$\begin{array}{r} 781 \\ +53 \\ \hline 7{,}134 \end{array}$$

   Ⓑ
   $$\begin{array}{r} 634 \\ +377 \\ \hline 1{,}011 \end{array}$$

   Ⓒ
   $$\begin{array}{r} 225 \\ +369 \\ \hline 694 \end{array}$$

   Ⓓ
   $$\begin{array}{r} 487 \\ +986 \\ \hline 1{,}463 \end{array}$$

4. Suppose that you are adding two 3-digit numbers. What is the greatest number of digits that could be in the sum?

   Ⓐ 3   Ⓑ 4   Ⓒ 5   Ⓓ 6

Go On   73

B. Solve each problem. Show all your work.

1. What is the sum of 317 miles and 79 miles?

2. Jim had 592 baseball cards. His sister Jill had 629 baseball cards. How many baseball cards did Jim and Jill have in all?

C. Complete the three parts below. Show all your work.

People at a shopping mall were asked to name their favorite food. Use the results shown in the table below to answer Parts A–C.

Burgers	Pizza	Tacos
63	235	176

Part A How many people named pizza or tacos as their favorite food?

Part B How many people named burgers or tacos as their favorite food?

Part C How many people in all named their favorite food?

SUBTRACTING WHOLE NUMBERS

This lesson addresses Benchmarks MA.A.3.2.2 and MA.A.3.2.3 of the Sunshine State Standards.

The Challenge

Jessica has 300 shells in her collection. She found 168 of the shells in California. She found the rest in Florida. How many shells in Jessica's collection are from Florida?

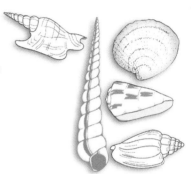

Learning the Ropes

To subtract two- and three-digit numbers, first write them in a column. Remember to line up the ones digits. Start at the right. First subtract the ones, then the tens, and finally the hundreds.

Always look at both digits in a column. Do you have a large enough number to subtract from? If not, you must regroup before you subtract. You can use addition to check that your difference is correct.

EXAMPLE Subtract 294 from 591.

STEP 1:

There are not enough ones to subtract from.

Regroup: 9 tens + 1 one
= 8 tens + 11 ones

$$\begin{array}{r} \overset{8\ 11}{5\cancel{9}\cancel{1}} \\ -294 \\ \hline 7 \end{array}$$

STEP 2:

There are not enough tens to subtract from.

Regroup: 5 hundreds + 8 tens
= 4 hundreds + 18 tens

$$\begin{array}{r} \overset{18}{\underset{}{}} \\ \overset{4\ \ 8\ 11}{\cancel{5}\cancel{9}\cancel{1}} \\ -294 \\ \hline 97 \end{array}$$

Steps continued on next page

Math in History

Calculating machines have been around for a long time! Blaise Pascal, a French mathematician, invented one of the first "arithmetic machines" in 1642. His machine used gears (notched wheels) that would move each time a number was added. The machine could add, subtract, multiply, and divide, but it worked by using addition only. Subtraction was done by using an addition fact from the same fact family.

Math in Use: Volunteer Work The Peace Corps is an organization that sends volunteers to work and teach in other countries. Many Peace Corps volunteers go to Africa. According to recent estimates, Tanzania has 105 volunteers, Kenya has 120, and Zimbabwe has 24. Ghana has 147 and Uganda has 8. How many more volunteers does Ghana have than Uganda? If there are a total of 110 volunteers in South Africa and Zimbabwe, how many volunteers does South Africa have?

STEP 3:
There are enough hundreds to subtract from.
Regrouping is not necessary.

$$
\begin{array}{r}
{\scriptstyle 18} \\
{\scriptstyle 4\,8\,11} \\
5\,9\,1 \\
-\,2\,9\,4 \\
\hline
2\,9\,7
\end{array}
$$

STEP 4:
Check by adding your answer to the number subtracted:

$$
\begin{array}{r}
{\scriptstyle 1\ 1} \\
2\,9\,7 \\
+\,2\,9\,4 \\
\hline
5\,9\,1
\end{array}
$$

Meeting the Challenge

To answer the Challenge, subtract the number of shells Jessica found in California from the total number of shells in her collection.

STEP 1:
There are no ones to subtract from and no tens to regroup.
Regroup: 3 hundreds + 0 tens = 2 hundreds + 10 tens

$$
\begin{array}{r}
{\scriptstyle 2\ 10} \\
3\,0\,0 \\
-\,1\,6\,8
\end{array}
$$

STEP 2:
Regroup:
10 tens + 0 ones = 9 tens + 10 ones

$$
\begin{array}{r}
{\scriptstyle 9} \\
{\scriptstyle 2\ 10\ 10} \\
3\,0\,0 \\
-\,1\,6\,8
\end{array}
$$

STEP 3:
Subtract the ones, tens, and hundreds.

$$
\begin{array}{r}
{\scriptstyle 9} \\
{\scriptstyle 2\ 10\ 10} \\
3\,0\,0 \\
-\,1\,6\,8 \\
\hline
1\,3\,2
\end{array}
$$

STEP 4:
Check by adding your answer to the number subtracted:

$$
\begin{array}{r}
{\scriptstyle 1\ 1} \\
1\,3\,2 \\
+\,1\,6\,8 \\
\hline
3\,0\,0
\end{array}
$$

Of the shells in Jessica's collection, 132 are from Florida.

Another Way You can use place-value models to help you subtract. Use 3 hundreds to show 300. Change one of the hundreds into 9 tens and 10 ones. Then cross out 1 hundred, 6 tens, and 8 ones, leaving 1 hundred, 3 tens, and 2 ones.

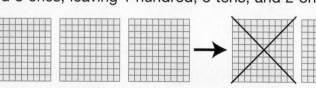

Name _____ Class _____ Date _____

Try It Yourself

A. Fill in the circle next to the correct answer to each multiple-choice question.

1. How many will be left if you take 85 away from 303?

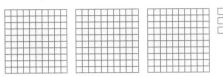

  Ⓐ 52   Ⓑ 118   Ⓒ 218   Ⓓ 245

2. Corey is reading a book that has 157 pages. He has already read 109 pages. How many pages does he have left to read?

  Ⓐ 42   Ⓑ 48   Ⓒ 52   Ⓓ 58

3. There are 423 students at Lake Center School. Of these, 84 students walk to school. The rest either take a bus or are driven to school. How many students ride to school?

  Ⓐ 461   Ⓑ 439   Ⓒ 349   Ⓓ 339

4. Beth is saving her money for an airline ticket that costs $500. So far, she has saved $436. How much more does she need?

  Ⓐ $164   Ⓑ $136   Ⓒ $64   Ⓓ $63

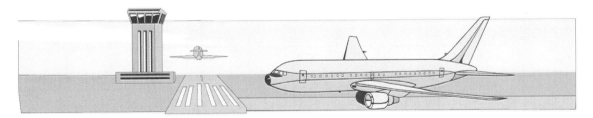

5. Cassie is going to visit her cousins. They live 483 miles away. After driving 178 miles, she stops at her grandparents' house. How much farther does Cassie have to drive?

  Ⓐ 260 miles   Ⓑ 305 miles   Ⓒ 315 miles   Ⓓ 661 miles

Go On ⮕

6. How many pounds heavier is a dog that weighs 115 pounds than a dog that weighs 59 pounds?

- Ⓐ 66 pounds
- Ⓑ 64 pounds
- Ⓒ 56 pounds
- Ⓓ 54 pounds

7. What number of people is 257 less than 902 people?

- Ⓐ 645 people
- Ⓑ 655 people
- Ⓒ 745 people
- Ⓓ 755 people

8. Which pair of numbers has the greatest difference?

- Ⓐ 27 and 139
- Ⓑ 27 and 603
- Ⓒ 139 and 495
- Ⓓ 495 and 603

9. Which must you do to subtract 28 from 135?

- Ⓐ Regroup 1 hundred and 3 tens as 13 ones.
- Ⓑ Regroup 3 tens as 30 ones.
- Ⓒ Regroup 13 ones as 1 ten and 3 ones.
- Ⓓ Regroup 3 tens and 5 ones as 2 tens and 15 ones.

10. Complete the two parts below. Show all your work.

Mary is taking a 500-mile bike trip.

Part A Mary has already biked 229 miles. How far does she have to go?

Part B Mary has been gone for 5 days so far. She has biked a different distance each day, but she always bikes between 40 and 50 miles. Tell how many miles she might have biked on each of the 5 days.

THE MEANING OF MULTIPLICATION

This lesson addresses Benchmarks MA.A.3.2.1, MA.A.3.2.2, and MA.A.5.2.1 of the Sunshine State Standards.

The Challenge

Mr. Hill packaged items for a bake sale at his children's school. He placed 4 cupcakes on each of 5 plates. He put 6 cookies in each of 7 bags.

How many cupcakes did he package? How many cookies did he package?

Math in History
For many years, the meat from Florida alligators has been sold. In 1997, about 56 tons of alligator meat were sold for about 14 thousand dollars per ton. In 1999, about 65 tons of alligator meat were sold for about 11 thousand dollars per ton. In which year was more money made selling alligator meat?

Learning the Ropes

You can use **multiplication** to find how many objects there are altogether in a number of equal groups. An **array** shows objects in rows and columns. Each row has the same number of objects. Each column has the same number of objects. This array contains 3 rows of 4 square tiles each.

$$4 + 4 + 4 = 12$$
$$3 \times 4 = 12$$
$$\uparrow \quad \uparrow \qquad \uparrow$$
factors   **product**

Remember that properties are the ways numbers behave. The **commutative property of multiplication** says that changing the order of the factors does not change the product.

EXAMPLE $2 \times 5 = 10$ $5 \times 2 = 10$

           2 groups of 5   5 groups of 2

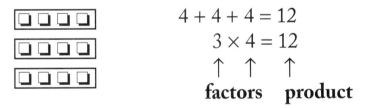

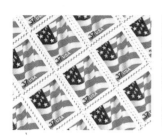

Math in Use: Stamps The U.S. Post Office sells stamps in booklets, on sheets, or in rolls. For example, you can buy sheets of 20 stamps. Each sheet has 5 rows of 4 stamps. How else might you arrange 20 stamps? You can also buy some stamps in sheets of 18 stamps. The sheet has 9 rows of 2 stamps. How else might you arrange 18 stamps?

The **associative property of multiplication** says that changing the way the factors are grouped does not change the product. (Count the arrows!)

EXAMPLE

$$(2 \times 3) \times 3$$
$$= \quad 6 \times 3$$
$$= \quad 18$$

$$2 \times (3 \times 3)$$
$$= 2 \times 9$$
$$= \quad 18$$

The **zero property of multiplication** says that any number times zero equals zero. For example, $4 \times 0 = 0$. The **identity property for multiplication** says that any number times 1 equals that number. For example, $5 \times 1 = 5$, and $1 \times 5 = 5$.

Meeting the Challenge

To answer the Challenge, you must find the total number of cupcakes and cookies. You can use multiplication because the cupcakes and cookies were packaged in equal groups.

Step 1: Find the total number of cupcakes. There were 4 cupcakes on each of 5 plates. Draw a picture or use a multiplication fact: $4 \times 5 = 20$.

Step 2: Find the total number of cookies. There were 6 cookies in each of 7 bags: $6 \times 7 = 42$.

Mr. Hill packaged 20 cupcakes and 42 cookies.

Another Way Another important property is the **distributive property of multiplication over addition,** which says that any number times the sum of two numbers equals the sum of that number times the first plus that number times the second.

EXAMPLE $\quad 3 \times (5 + 2) \quad = \quad 3 \times 5 \ + \ 3 \times 2 \quad = \quad 21$

Name _____ Class _____ Date _____

Try It Yourself

A. Fill in the circle next to the correct answer to each multiple-choice question.

1. Which multiplication sentence is represented by this number line?

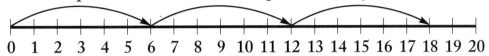

0 1 2 3 4 5 6 7 8 9 10 11 12 13 14 15 16 17 18 19 20

Ⓐ $3 \times 5 = 18$ Ⓑ $6 + 12 = 18$ Ⓒ $3 \times 6 = 18$ Ⓓ $6 + 6 + 6 = 18$

2. Molly can put 4 photos on each page of her photo album. So far, she has filled 7 album pages. Which number sentence shows how many photos Molly has put in her album?

Ⓐ $4 + 7 = 11$ Ⓑ $7 - 4 = 3$ Ⓒ $7 \times 4 = 28$ Ⓓ $4 \times 7 = 47$

3. There are 9 players on a baseball team. Which number sentence shows the number of players needed to form 4 teams?

Ⓐ $4 + 9 = 13$ Ⓑ $4 \times 9 = 36$ Ⓒ $9 - 5 = 4$ Ⓓ $4 \times 9 = 27$

4. Which number will make this sentence true?

$(4 \times 2) \times 3 = 4 \times (\underline{} \times 3)$

Ⓐ 4   Ⓑ 3   Ⓒ 2   Ⓓ 1

5. Which sentence is NOT true?

Ⓐ $0 \times 7 = 0$ Ⓑ $6 \times 1 = 6$ Ⓒ $1 \times 1 = 1$ Ⓓ $8 \times 0 = 8$

6. Which array represents 2×8?

Ⓐ ❄❄❄❄❄❄❄❄❄❄
     ❄❄❄❄❄❄❄❄❄❄

Ⓒ   ❄❄
     ❄❄❄❄❄❄❄❄

Ⓑ ❄❄❄❄❄❄❄❄❄
     ❄❄❄❄❄❄❄❄❄

Ⓓ ❄❄❄❄
     ❄❄❄❄

Go On →

7. Marvin is fixing breakfast for 20 people. He is preparing orange juice for the breakfast. For each can of frozen orange juice, he needs to add 3 cans of water. He uses 4 cans of frozen orange juice. Which number sentence shows how many cans of water he should add?

(A) $20 \times 3 = 60$ (B) $20 \times 4 = 80$ (C) $3 \times 4 = 12$ (D) $4 + 3 = 7$

8. There are 5 people in the Williams family. Each person wears 1 pair of socks (2 socks) every day. Which number sentence shows how many socks have to be washed each week (7 days)?

(A) $5 \times 1 \times 2 = 10$ (C) $5 \times 1 \times 7 = 35$

(B) $1 \times 2 \times 7 = 14$ (D) $5 \times 2 \times 7 = 70$

9. Complete the two parts below. Use your own paper.

The chart below shows the products when 9 is multiplied by each of the numbers from 1 to 10.

×	1	2	3	4	5	6	7	8	9	10
9	9	18	27	36	45	54	63	72	81	90

Part A What do you notice about the sum of the digits of each product?

Part B Study the chart above and the diagram below. With each new product, the ones digit decreases by 1. What happens to the tens digit?

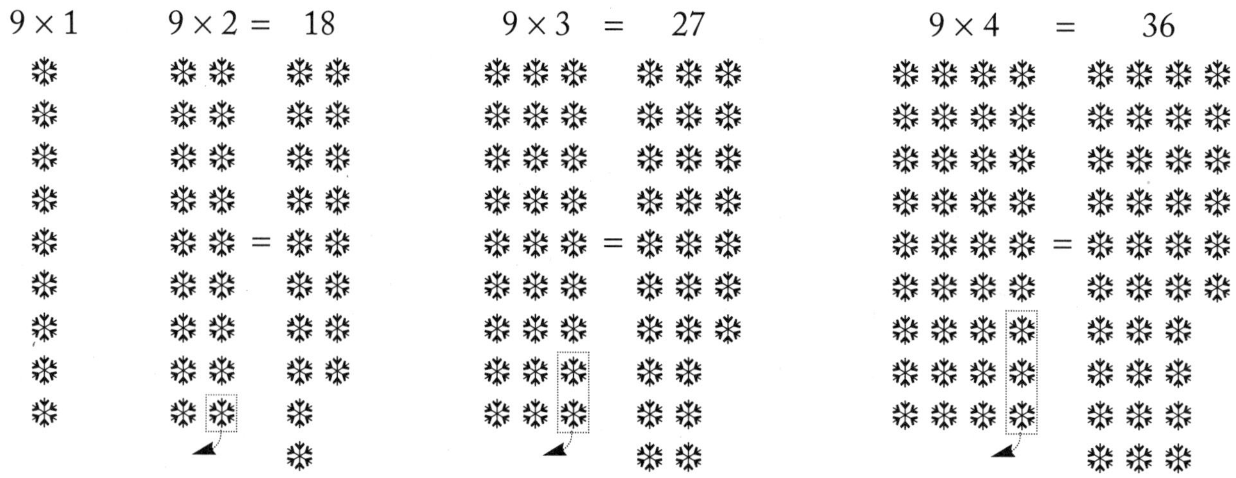

MULTIPLYING WHOLE NUMBERS

This lesson addresses Benchmarks MA.A.3.2.2 and MA.A.3.2.3 of the Sunshine State Standards.

Math in History
The record speed for a car was about 40 miles per hour in 1898. By 1906, the speed record was three times as fast. By 1938, the speed record was 9 times as fast. Recent speed records are held by jet-powered cars. The 1997 speed record is about 9 times the 85-miles-per-hour rate from 1903. Use multiplication to find the land-speed records in 1906, 1938, and 1997.

The Challenge

One airline makes 8 flights each day from Tampa to San Antonio. Each flight can carry 267 passengers. How many passengers can this airline fly to San Antonio each day?

Learning the Ropes

You can use place-value models to multiply whole numbers.

EXAMPLE Find the product of 29 and 3.

Here is a place-value model of 29 (2 tens and 9 ones):

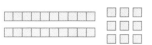

To multiply 29 by 3, you have to multiply both the ones and the tens by 3:

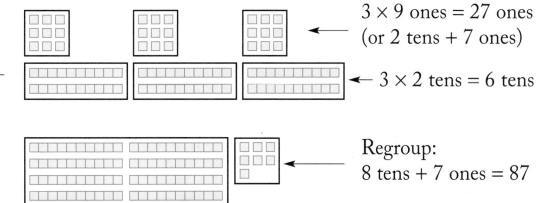

3×9 ones = 27 ones
(or 2 tens + 7 ones)

3×2 tens = 6 tens

Regroup:
8 tens + 7 ones = 87

The steps for this process are shown on the next page.

Math in Use: Environment Recycling one aluminum can saves enough energy to run a television for 3 hours. You can use multiplication to find out how long you could run a television if you recycled 14 cans. Recycling one glass bottle saves enough energy to light a 100-watt bulb for 4 hours. How long could you burn that light bulb if everyone in your class or school recycled a bottle?

STEP 1:
Multiply the ones:
$3 \times 9 = 27$
Regroup: 27 ones =
2 tens + 7 ones

$$\begin{array}{r} {\scriptstyle 2} \\ 2\,9 \\ \times\ \ 3 \\ \hline 7 \end{array}$$

STEP 2:
Multiply the tens:
$3 \times 2 = 6$
Add all the tens:
6 tens + 2 tens = 8 tens

$$\begin{array}{r} {\scriptstyle 2} \\ 2\,9 \\ \times\ \ 3 \\ \hline 8\,7 \end{array}$$

Meeting the Challenge

To answer the Challenge, you need to multiply a 3-digit number by a 1-digit number. Start at the right, and multiply each digit of the 3-digit number by the 1-digit number.

STEP 1:
Multiply the ones:
$8 \times 7 = 56$
Regroup: 56 ones =
5 tens + 6 ones

$$\begin{array}{r} {\scriptstyle 5} \\ 2\,6\,7 \\ \times\ \ 8 \\ \hline 6 \end{array}$$

STEP 2:
Multiply the tens:
$8 \times 6 = 48$
Add all the tens:
$48 + 5 = 53$
Regroup: 53 tens =
5 hundreds + 3 tens

$$\begin{array}{r} {\scriptstyle 5\ 5} \\ 2\,6\,7 \\ \times\ \ 8 \\ \hline 3\,6 \end{array}$$

STEP 3:
Multiply the hundreds:
$8 \times 2 = 16$
Add all the hundreds:
$16 + 5 = 21$
Regroup: 21 hundreds =
2 thousands + 1 hundred

$$\begin{array}{r} {\scriptstyle 5\ 5} \\ 2\,6\,7 \\ \times\ \ 8 \\ \hline 2{,}1\,3\,6 \end{array}$$

The airline can fly 2,136 passengers from Tampa to San Antonio each day.

Another Way Here is another way to multiply 3×29. First, find the product of 3 times the ones ($3 \times 9 = 27$). Then, find the product of 3 times the tens ($3 \times 20 = 60$). Finally, add the products together ($27 + 60 = 87$).

$$\begin{array}{r} 29 \\ \times\ \ 3 \\ \hline 27\ {\scriptstyle (3 \times 9)} \\ +\,60\ {\scriptstyle (3 \times 20)} \\ \hline 87 \end{array}$$

Try It Yourself

A. Fill in the circle next to the correct answer to each multiple-choice question.

1. The cost of an adult ticket to one amusement park is $17. What is the total cost of 4 adult tickets?

   Ⓐ $ 21

   Ⓑ $ 48

   Ⓒ $ 68

   Ⓓ $174

2. Jackson has 5 rolls of quarters. Each roll has 40 quarters. How many quarters does Jackson have?

   Ⓐ 8   Ⓑ 35   Ⓒ 45   Ⓓ 200

3. Mr. Morgan drives 36 miles each day back and forth to work. Each week he works five days—Monday through Friday. How many miles (mi) does he drive altogether to and from work in one week?

   Ⓐ 72 mi   Ⓑ 150 mi   Ⓒ 153 mi   Ⓓ 180 mi

4. Dustin was helping to set up chairs for the school band concert. Nine rows of 43 chairs each were needed. How many chairs had to be set up in all?

   Ⓐ 377   Ⓑ 386   Ⓒ 387   Ⓓ 3,627

5. The cost of a round-trip airline ticket from Fort Lauderdale to Philadelphia on one airline is $299. What is the total cost of 5 round-trip tickets to Philadelphia on this airline?

   Ⓐ $1,055   Ⓑ $1,445   Ⓒ $1,455   Ⓓ $1,495

Go On

6. Ms. Chan asked her students to multiply 523 by 4. The work done by four students is shown. Which student worked the problem correctly?

Ⓐ Angie:
$$
\begin{array}{r}
1 \\
5\,2\,3 \\
\times \quad 4 \\
\hline
2,1\,8\,2
\end{array}
$$

Ⓒ Jacob:
$$
\begin{array}{r}
1 \\
5\,2\,3 \\
\times \quad 4 \\
\hline
2,0\,9\,2
\end{array}
$$

Ⓑ Alex:
$$
\begin{array}{r}
11 \\
5\,2\,3 \\
\times \quad 4 \\
\hline
2,1\,9\,2
\end{array}
$$

Ⓓ Merri:
$$
\begin{array}{r}
1 \\
5\,2\,3 \\
\times \quad 4 \\
\hline
2,0\,7\,2
\end{array}
$$

7. Each machine shipped by one company weighs 217 pounds (lb). What is the total weight of a shipment of 7 machines?

Ⓐ 1,979 lb   Ⓑ 1,519 lb   Ⓒ 1,517 lb   Ⓓ 1,479 lb

8. Complete the problem below. Show all your work.

On Farmer Fender's farm there are 6 spiders, each with 8 legs. There are also 6 chickens, each with 2 legs, and 6 sheep, each with 4 legs. If you count the legs on all the spiders, chickens, and sheep, how many legs are there?

THE MEANING OF DIVISION

This lesson addresses Benchmarks MA.A.3.2.1 and MA.A.3.2.2 of the Sunshine State Standards.

The Challenge

Timor has 54 sports cards to place in his card album. He can place 9 cards on each page. He buys pages in sets of 3. How many sets of pages does he need for the cards?

Learning the Ropes

You can use **division** to find how many equal groups. You can also use division to find how many are in each equal group.

EXAMPLE If you put 18 counters into groups of 3, how many groups could you make?

Start with 18 counters. Draw rings around groups of 3.

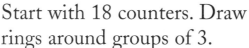

If you divide 18 counters into groups of 3, you can make 6 groups: $18 \div 3 = 6$.

EXAMPLE If you put 18 counters into 3 equal groups, how many would be in each group?

Draw 3 rings. Put the same number of counters in each ring until you have used 18 counters.

If you divide 18 counters into 3 groups, there will be 6 in each group: $18 \div 3 = 6$.

The parts of a division problem have special names:

18	÷	3	=	6
dividend		**divisor**		**quotient**

Math in History
The United States has had many different flag designs since 1777. The 13 stripes have stayed the same since 1812, but the star pattern has changed as new states have joined the Union. From 1822 to 1836, our flag had 24 stars (4 rows of 6 stars). What are the multiplication and division facts for 24, 4, and 6? How might the 30 stars in the 1848 flag have been arranged? What about the 48 stars on the 1912 flag?

Unit 1: Number Sense, Concepts, and Operations   **87**

Math in Use: Health Athletes who do long-distance running know the importance of drinking lots of fluids while running. On long runs, it is a good idea to drink every 2 miles or so. About how many drinks should a runner have during a marathon (a 26-mile race)? Divide 26 miles by 2; the quotient is 13. A marathon runner should drink about 13 times during the race.

Division is the opposite of multiplication. A **fact family** includes the multiplication and division facts that use the same numbers.

$3 \times 6 = 18$	$18 \div 6 = 3$
$6 \times 3 = 18$	$18 \div 3 = 6$

There are special rules for division using the numbers zero and one.

- The quotient of *any number divided by one is that number.* If you put 6 coins into 1 group, there are 6 coins in the group ($6 \div 1 = 6$).
- The quotient of *any number divided by itself is one.* For example, if you divide 6 coins into 6 equal groups, there is 1 coin in each group ($6 \div 6 = 1$).
- The quotient of *zero divided by any number is zero.* If you divide zero coins into 6 groups, there are zero coins in each group ($0 \div 6 = 0$).
- You cannot divide by zero.

Meeting the Challenge

To answer the Challenge, divide to find the number of pages Timor needs. Then divide again to find the number of sets of pages he needs.

Step 1: Timor has 54 cards. He can fit 9 cards on each page. Use a division fact to find the number of pages he needs. You can also draw a picture or model.

Step 2: Timor needs 6 pages. He buys pages in sets of 3. Use another division fact to find how many sets he needs: $6 \div 3 = 2$.

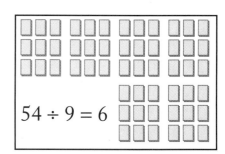

$54 \div 9 = 6$

Timor needs 2 sets of pages (6 pages in all) for his cards.

Another Way You can also use arrays to show how to divide numbers. To show how to divide 18 by 3 or by 6, you can draw an array of 18 squares arranged in 3 rows. There are 3 rows of 6 squares each.

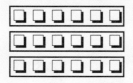

$18 \div 3 = 6$

$18 \div 6 = 3$

Name _____ Class _____ Date _____

Try It Yourself

A. Fill in the circle next to the correct answer to each multiple-choice question.

1. Which number sentence is NOT shown by this array?

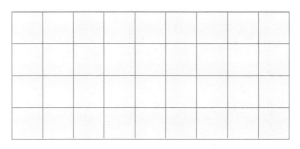

   Ⓐ $36 \div 9 = 4$ Ⓑ $4 \times 9 = 36$ Ⓒ $36 \div 4 = 9$ Ⓓ $36 \times 4 = 204$

2. The 20 students in Lia's class sit in rows of 5 students each. In how many rows do the students sit?

   Ⓐ 4   Ⓑ 5   Ⓒ 15   Ⓓ 100

3. Each box on the scale shown contains the same item. What is the weight (in pounds) of one box?

   Ⓐ 72 lb
   Ⓑ 24 lb
   Ⓒ 8 lb
   Ⓓ 7 lb

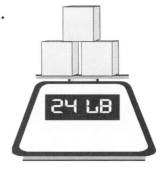

4. Which statement is true?

   Ⓐ $0 \div 4 = 4$ Ⓑ $4 \div 4 = 0$ Ⓒ $4 \div 1 = 1$ Ⓓ $4 \div 4 = 1$

5. Which situation is NOT represented by the number sentence $16 \div 8 = 2$?

   Ⓐ 16 objects are arranged in groups of 8.
   Ⓑ There are 2 groups of 8 objects each.
   Ⓒ Objects are arranged in 8 groups of 16 each.
   Ⓓ 16 objects are arranged in 8 equal groups.

Go On ⟩

6. Which fact is NOT in the fact family for 3, 7, and 21?

Ⓐ $21 \div 7 = 3$ Ⓑ $3 \times 7 = 21$ Ⓒ $63 \div 3 = 21$ Ⓓ $7 \times 3 = 21$

7. A number is **even** if it is equal to two times a number. For example, 6 is even because $6 = 2 \times 3$. A number is **odd** if it is one more than an even number. Which list below contains *only* even numbers?

Ⓐ 4, 6, 8, 10   Ⓑ 4, 7, 10, 13   Ⓒ 3, 7, 11, 15   Ⓓ 2, 3, 4, 5

8. Complete the three parts below. Show all your work. Use your own paper.

The table below shows the pieces of fruit that Greg plans to put in each holiday fruit basket he is making. Use the table to answer Parts A–C.

HOLIDAY FRUIT BASKETS	
Fruit	**Number of Pieces**
Apples	5
Bananas	3
Oranges	6
Pears	4

Part A Greg buys a case of 36 oranges. How many baskets can he make with these oranges?

Part B A bag of bananas contains 15 bananas. How many baskets can be filled with these bananas?

Part C Greg picks 35 apples off the trees in his family's yard. How many baskets can he fill with these apples?

ROUNDING WHOLE NUMBERS

This lesson addresses Benchmark MA.A.4.2.1 of the Sunshine State Standards.

Math in History
Throughout history, most calendars have been based on the seasons and the Earth's movements. A year is the time it takes the Earth to circle the sun. How long is a year? Astronomers calculate a year as 365 days, 5 hours, 48 minutes, and 46 seconds. Our calendar year of 365 days is a rounded number. The "extra" part of a day (almost 6 hours) can be rounded to a full extra day (24 hours) every four years. The years with an extra day are called **leap years.**

The Challenge

When Megan arrived at the museum, there were already 253 people in line for the fossil exhibit. She had to wait 42 minutes.

To the nearest hundred, how many people were in line? To the nearest ten, how many minutes did Megan have to wait?

Learning the Ropes

There are times when you don't need an exact number. You can use **rounding** to get a number that is close enough to the real number.

A number line can help you find a number that is close to the real number.

EXAMPLE   Round 38 to the nearest ten.

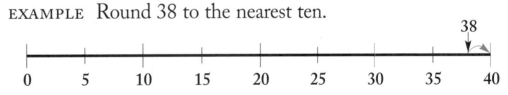

The number 38 is between 30 and 40, but it is closer to 40.

EXAMPLE   Round 229 to the nearest hundred.

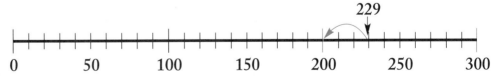

The number 229 is between 200 and 300 but closer to 200.

If the number is halfway between two rounded numbers, round up to the higher number. For example, 150 is halfway between 100 and 200, so round it up to 200.

These rules will help you to round numbers without drawing number lines.

- Look at the digit to the right of the place you are rounding.
- If the digit to its right is *less than 5* (< 5), **round down** (keep the digit to be rounded the same).
- If the digit to its right is *greater than or equal to 5* (≥ 5), **round up** (increase the digit to be rounded by 1).
- Other digits to the right become zero.

EXAMPLE Round 371 to the nearest hundred.

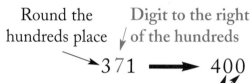

Round the hundreds place   Digit to the right of the hundreds

371 ⟶ 400

7 ≥ 5, so round up and put in zeros.

Meeting the Challenge

To answer the Challenge, round the number of people in line to the nearest hundred and the minutes Megan waited to the nearest ten.

STEP 1: Round 253 to the nearest hundred.
You are rounding the hundreds place. ⟶ 253
Look at the digit to the right of the hundreds place. ⟶ 253   5 ≥ 5
Round up and put in zeros. ⟶ 300

STEP 2: Round 42 to the nearest ten. The digit next to the tens place (2) is less than 5, so round down to 40.

To the nearest hundred, there were 300 people in line. To the nearest ten, Megan had to wait for 40 minutes.

Another Way You can also use place-value models to help you round. To round 42 to the nearest ten, use models to show 40 and 50, because 42 is between 40 and 50.

40   42   50

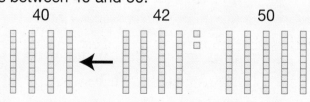

Try It Yourself

A. Fill in the circle next to the correct answer to each multiple-choice question.

1. A football player weighs 284 pounds (lb). Round his weight to the nearest hundred pounds.

   Ⓐ 200 lb   Ⓑ 280 lb   Ⓒ 300 lb   Ⓓ 800 lb

2. There are 46 children who ride Anna's school bus. Round this number to the nearest ten.

   Ⓐ 40   Ⓑ 45   Ⓒ 46   Ⓓ 50

3. Renaldo told his parents that he wants a bike that costs about $200. If this price has been rounded to the nearest hundred dollars, which of these could be the exact price of the bike?

   Ⓐ $135   Ⓑ $149   Ⓒ $217   Ⓓ $262

4. Which of these numbers does NOT round to 80?

   Ⓐ 85   Ⓑ 83   Ⓒ 79   Ⓓ 75

5. What is the largest number that rounds to 30?

   Ⓐ 29   Ⓑ 34   Ⓒ 35   Ⓓ 39

6. What is the smallest number that rounds to 600?

   Ⓐ 601   Ⓑ 560   Ⓒ 551   Ⓓ 550

7. It is 352 miles (mi) from Hector's home to his grandparents' home. Round this distance to the nearest hundred miles.

   Ⓐ 300 mi   Ⓑ 350 mi   Ⓒ 360 mi   Ⓓ 400 mi

Go On ⇨

8. The number of third graders at Vernon School, rounded to the nearest ten, is 60. What are all the possible numbers of third graders at this school?

Ⓐ 51 to 69　　　Ⓑ 55 to 64　　　Ⓒ 56 to 65　　　Ⓓ 61 to 64

9. The students in Tina's class collected 709 cans for recycling. Tina is writing an article for the school newspaper about this. Which is the best headline for Tina to use for her article?

Ⓐ "Class Collects 700 Cans"　　　Ⓒ "Class Collects 800 Cans"

Ⓑ "Class Collects 750 Cans"　　　Ⓓ "Class Collects 900 Cans"

10. Kayla has cards for the digits 2, 4, and 6. She arranges the cards to form numbers. Which number rounds up when rounded to the nearest hundred?

Ⓐ 246　　　Ⓑ 264　　　Ⓒ 426　　　Ⓓ 642

11. To the nearest hundred, Gary has about 500 coins in his collection. What could be the exact number of coins in his collection?

Ⓐ 591　　　Ⓑ 550　　　Ⓒ 461　　　Ⓓ 449

12. Complete the three parts below. Show all your work.

The price of a computer, rounded to the nearest hundred dollars, is $900. The printer that goes with it costs $400, to the nearest hundred dollars.

Part A What is the lowest possible price of this computer? What is the highest price?

Part B What is the lowest possible price of the printer? What is the highest price?

Part C The total price rounds to $1,300. What is the lowest possible price of the computer and printer? What is the highest price?

ESTIMATING SUMS AND DIFFERENCES

This lesson addresses Benchmark MA.A.4.2.1 of the Sunshine State Standards.

The Challenge

The students at Sam Houston Elementary School had a canned food drive. The table shows how much was collected during each week of the drive.

About how many more cans were collected during the last week than during the first week? About how many cans of food were collected in all?

CANNED FOOD DRIVE	
Week	**Cans Collected**
1	283
2	452
3	729

Math in History
In 1842, Lansford Hastings made the long journey to the West. He wrote a book about going west. In his book, he told people to bring at least 200 pounds of flour, 150 pounds of bacon, 10 pounds of salt, 20 pounds of sugar, and 10 pounds of coffee. But some travelers carried too much! They over-estimated the amount of weight that their wagons could carry. They had to throw out food along the way.

Learning the Ropes

Sometimes you do not need an exact answer to an addition or subtraction problem. You can **estimate** the sum or difference. That means you find a number that is close to the exact answer.

To estimate, first round each number so that it has one or more zeros at the end. Then you can add or subtract in your head.

EXAMPLES   Estimate these answers.

$$39 + 54 = ?$$

$$
\begin{array}{r}
39 \\
+54 \\
\end{array}
\longrightarrow
\begin{array}{r}
40 \\
+50 \\
\hline
90 \\
\end{array}
$$

$$921 - 446 = ?$$

$$
\begin{array}{r}
921 \\
-446 \\
\end{array}
\longrightarrow
\begin{array}{r}
900 \\
-400 \\
\hline
500 \\
\end{array}
$$

39 + 54 is about 90.

921 − 446 is about 500.

Math in Use: Estimating Costs How much do you think it would cost to keep a puppy for the first year? Food can cost between $100 and $400 a year, depending on the dog's size. Your puppy will also need to go to the vet for shots and other treatment to keep it healthy. This can cost more than $600 for the first year. Your family's expenses would be $700 to $1,000 so far. Your puppy will also need a license, along with bigger collars and leashes as it grows. Don't forget training classes and toys.

You can also use estimation and rounding to check whether an exact answer is **reasonable** (could be right).

EXAMPLES   Check these answers.

$$
\begin{array}{r}
429 + 753 = 1{,}182 \\
\begin{array}{r}
429 \longrightarrow 400 \\
+753 \longrightarrow +800 \\
\hline
1{,}182 \qquad 1{,}200
\end{array}
\end{array}
\quad \text{Check}
$$

1,182 rounds to 1,200,
so 1,182 is reasonable.

$$
\begin{array}{r}
789 - 411 = 378 \\
\begin{array}{r}
789 \longrightarrow 800 \\
-411 \longrightarrow -400 \\
\hline
378 \qquad 400
\end{array}
\end{array}
\quad \text{Check}
$$

378 rounds to 400,
so 378 is reasonable.

Meeting the Challenge

To answer the Challenge, estimate to find answers that are close.

STEP 1: To estimate how many more cans were collected during the last week than during the first week, round the numbers of cans collected during Weeks 1 and 3. Then, find the difference of the rounded numbers.

$$
\begin{array}{r}
729 \longrightarrow 700 \\
-283 \longrightarrow -300 \\
\hline
400
\end{array}
$$

STEP 2: To estimate the total number of cans collected, round the number of cans collected each week. Then, find the sum of the rounded numbers.

$$
\begin{array}{r}
283 \longrightarrow 300 \\
452 \longrightarrow 500 \\
+729 \longrightarrow +700 \\
\hline
1{,}500
\end{array}
$$

About 400 more cans were collected during the last week than during the first week of the drive. Altogether, about 1,500 cans were collected.

Another Way You can also use **front-end estimation** to estimate a sum or difference. Keep the front digit of each number and write zeros for the other digits. Then add or subtract the numbers.

EXAMPLES

$$
\begin{array}{r}
729 \rightarrow 700 \\
-283 \rightarrow -200 \\
\hline
500
\end{array}
\qquad
\begin{array}{r}
452 \rightarrow 400 \\
+729 \rightarrow +700 \\
\hline
1{,}100
\end{array}
$$

Name _____ Class _____ Date _____

Try It Yourself

A. Fill in the circle next to the correct answer to each multiple-choice question.

1. For which situation is an exact sum or difference needed?
   - Ⓐ Do you have enough money to buy all 10 items at the grocery store?
   - Ⓑ How much change should you get back from a store clerk?
   - Ⓒ Which plane flight is more expensive?
   - Ⓓ How much money should your class try to raise to cover the cost of a field trip?

2. Maria's school bus can seat 57 students. At one stop, 24 students board the bus. Using rounding, what is the best estimate of how many seats are still available on the bus?
   - Ⓐ 20   Ⓑ 40   Ⓒ 80   Ⓓ 100

3. The Cooks went on vacation. They drove 132 miles the first day, 97 miles the second day, and 380 miles the third day. About how many miles did the Cooks drive in these three days? Choose the answer below that shows the best way to estimate this distance using rounding.
   - Ⓐ 100 + 100 + 400
   - Ⓑ 100 + 90 + 300
   - Ⓒ 132 + 97 + 380
   - Ⓓ 400 − 100

4. When rounding is used, what is the best estimate of 973 − 256?
   - Ⓐ 600   Ⓑ 700   Ⓒ 800   Ⓓ 1,200

5. Scott used rounding to estimate the sum of 27 and 39. Which statement could Scott correctly make about this sum?
   - Ⓐ The sum is less than 50.
   - Ⓑ The sum is less than 60.
   - Ⓒ The sum is less than 70.
   - Ⓓ The sum is greater than 70.

Go On ⟩

6. Julia went shopping at the Clothes Rack. The prices of four items that she liked are shown in the table. The best estimate of what Julia spent at the Clothes Rack is $70. Which pair of items might Julia have bought?

Ⓐ shoes and T-shirt

Ⓑ T-shirt and sweater

Ⓒ jeans and sweater

Ⓓ jeans and T-shirt

CLOTHES RACK PRICES	
Jeans	$23
Shoes	$49
T-Shirt	$18
Sweater	$34

7. Complete the three parts below. Show all your work.

Three members of the Science Club were comparing their insect collections. Use the table to the right to make your estimates for Parts A–C. Round to the nearest hundred.

INSECT COLLECTIONS	
Name	**Number of Insects**
Brittany	316
Franklin	487
Peng	171

Part A If Brittany and Peng combined their collections, what is the best estimate of how many insects they would have in the new collection?

Part B What is the best estimate of how many more insects are in the largest collection than in the smallest collection?

Part C What is the best estimate of how many insects Brittany, Franklin, and Peng have in all?

FRACTIONS

This lesson addresses Benchmarks MA.A.1.2.1, MA.A.1.2.2, MA.A.1.2.3, and MA.A.1.2.4 of the Sunshine State Standards.

The Challenge

Brad lives $\frac{4}{5}$ mile from school. He lives $\frac{7}{10}$ mile from the soccer field. Does Brad live closer to school or to the soccer field?

Learning the Ropes

Fractions can be used to describe part of a whole or some of a group. The **numerator,** or top number of a fraction, tells how many parts are being used. The **denominator,** or bottom number, tells how many equal parts are in the whole or in the group:

numerator → $\frac{3}{8}$ ← parts used
denominator → ← equal parts in all

Both of the models here show $\frac{3}{8}$, which is read "three-eighths."

Equivalent fractions name the same amount. The fraction bars here show that $\frac{1}{2}$, $\frac{2}{4}$, $\frac{3}{6}$, and $\frac{4}{8}$ are all equivalent.

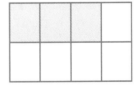

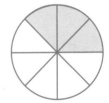

$\frac{1}{2}$				$\frac{1}{2}$			
$\frac{1}{4}$		$\frac{1}{4}$		$\frac{1}{4}$		$\frac{1}{4}$	
$\frac{1}{6}$	$\frac{1}{6}$	$\frac{1}{6}$		$\frac{1}{6}$	$\frac{1}{6}$	$\frac{1}{6}$	
$\frac{1}{8}$	$\frac{1}{8}$	$\frac{1}{8}$	$\frac{1}{8}$	$\frac{1}{8}$	$\frac{1}{8}$	$\frac{1}{8}$	$\frac{1}{8}$

Math in History
Fractions have been used for nearly 4,000 years. The use of fractions is shown in the Rhind Papyrus. This ancient "book" was written in Egypt around 1650 B.C. The Rhind Papyrus had 87 puzzle-type problems. One problem asked how to divide a loaf of bread among 10 people. Another asked how to divide 2 loaves among 10 people, and so on, up to 9 loaves. In these problems, the Egyptians were making the fractions $\frac{1}{10}$, $\frac{2}{10}$, and so on.

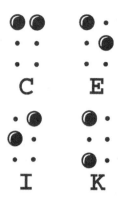

Math in Use: Braille People who cannot see words on a page can read with their fingers. In 1826, Louis Braille of France created symbols for letters and numbers using raised dots. Each set of 6 dots has 3 rows of 2 dots. Some dots are raised, and some are flat. You can tell which letter or number it is by which dots are raised and which are flat. Five different arrangements have 2 out of the 6 dots raised. Another way to say this is that $\frac{2}{6}$, or $\frac{1}{3}$, of the dots are raised. The letter c has two raised dots in the top row. How many other ways can $\frac{1}{3}$ of the dots be raised?

You can compare fractions to compare parts of a whole or parts of a group.

EXAMPLES   Compare the following fractions: $\frac{3}{10}$ and $\frac{9}{10}$ $\frac{3}{4}$ and $\frac{2}{5}$

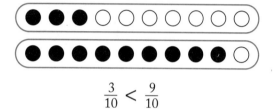

$$\frac{3}{10} < \frac{9}{10}$$

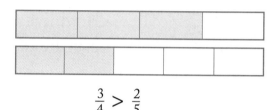

$$\frac{3}{4} > \frac{2}{5}$$

Meeting the Challenge

To answer the Challenge, compare $\frac{4}{5}$ and $\frac{7}{10}$.

STEP 1: Draw models of $\frac{4}{5}$ and $\frac{7}{10}$.

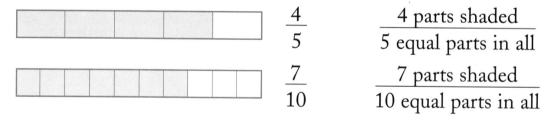

$$\frac{4}{5} \qquad \frac{\text{4 parts shaded}}{\text{5 equal parts in all}}$$

$$\frac{7}{10} \qquad \frac{\text{7 parts shaded}}{\text{10 equal parts in all}}$$

STEP 2: Compare the shaded areas of the models. More of the model for $\frac{4}{5}$ is shaded than of the model for $\frac{7}{10}$. Thus, $\frac{4}{5} > \frac{7}{10}$.

Because $\frac{7}{10}$ mile is less than $\frac{4}{5}$ mile, Brad lives closer to the soccer field.

Another Way You can also compare the fractions in the Challenge using the box method. On a sheet of graph paper, make two rectangles. Let the length and width of each rectangle be the denominators. Shade 4 rows out of 5, and 7 columns out of 10. The one with more shaded boxes is larger.

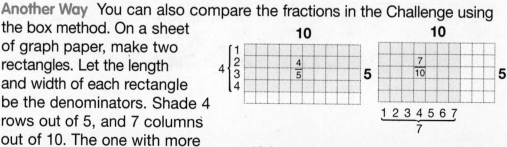

40 boxes > 35 boxes, so $\frac{4}{5} > \frac{7}{10}$.

Name _____   Class _____   Date _____

Try It Yourself

A. Fill in the circle next to the correct answer to each multiple-choice question.

1. Which model shows $\frac{2}{5}$ shaded?

   Ⓐ    Ⓑ    Ⓒ    Ⓓ

2. Lori has 3 dogs and 7 cats in her stuffed animal collection. She has no other kinds of animals in her collection. What part of Lori's stuffed animal collection are cats?

   Ⓐ $\frac{3}{10}$ Ⓑ $\frac{4}{7}$ Ⓒ $\frac{7}{3}$ Ⓓ $\frac{7}{10}$

3. Alicia has four pizzas that are the same size. She cuts each pizza into different-sized pieces. Which pizza has the largest pieces?

   Ⓐ the pizza that is cut into eighths

   Ⓑ the pizza that is cut into ninths

   Ⓒ the pizza that is cut into sixths

   Ⓓ the pizza that is cut into twelfths

4. Ben and Kari both have the same number of math problems to do for homework. Ben finished $\frac{5}{8}$ of his homework. Kari finished $\frac{1}{2}$ of her homework. Which statement is true?

   Ⓐ Ben and Kari finished the same number of problems.

   Ⓑ Ben finished more problems than Kari.

   Ⓒ Kari finished more problems than Ben.

   Ⓓ Ben has done all his homework.

Go On

Use the models to the right to answer questions 5 and 6.

$\frac{1}{3}$		$\frac{1}{3}$		$\frac{1}{3}$	
$\frac{1}{6}$	$\frac{1}{6}$	$\frac{1}{6}$	$\frac{1}{6}$	$\frac{1}{6}$	$\frac{1}{6}$

$\frac{1}{9}$	$\frac{1}{9}$	$\frac{1}{9}$	$\frac{1}{9}$	$\frac{1}{9}$	$\frac{1}{9}$	$\frac{1}{9}$	$\frac{1}{9}$	$\frac{1}{9}$

$\frac{1}{12}$	$\frac{1}{12}$	$\frac{1}{12}$	$\frac{1}{12}$	$\frac{1}{12}$	$\frac{1}{12}$	$\frac{1}{12}$	$\frac{1}{12}$	$\frac{1}{12}$	$\frac{1}{12}$	$\frac{1}{12}$	$\frac{1}{12}$

5. Which number sentence is true?

(A) $\frac{2}{3} > \frac{8}{9}$

(C) $\frac{6}{9} = \frac{1}{3}$

(B) $\frac{4}{6} = \frac{8}{12}$

(D) $\frac{9}{12} < \frac{4}{6}$

6. Which number sentence is true?

(A) $\frac{1}{3} = \frac{3}{12}$

(B) $\frac{10}{12} > \frac{7}{9}$

(C) $\frac{4}{6} = \frac{7}{9}$

(D) $\frac{3}{6} = \frac{1}{3}$

B. Complete the three parts below. Show all your work.

Use this set of shapes to answer Parts A–C.

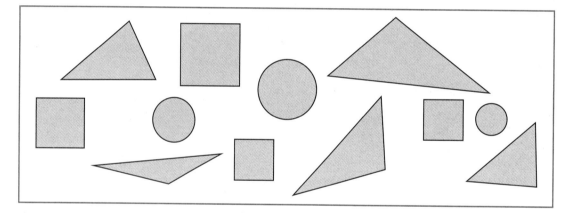

Part A In the numerator of the fraction to the right, write the number of circles in the box. In the denominator, write the number of shapes altogether. The fraction you have made shows what fraction of the group of shapes are circles. What fraction of the group are circles?

Part B What fraction of the group of shapes have straight sides?

Part C What fraction of the group of shapes are NOT triangles?

102 AIM Higher! FCAT Mathematics

Name _____ Class _____ Date _____

1. Mrs. Corrigan's class is collecting cans for a food drive. The students get 2 points for each small can they bring in. They get 3 points for each large can. The table below shows the number of small and large cans brought in each day.

Unit 1

Day	Number of Small Cans	Number of Large Cans	Number of Points
Monday	1	2	2 + 6 = 8
Tuesday	3	3	
Wednesday	3	4	
Thursday	2	1	
Friday	4	3	
TOTAL			

Part A Fill in the table to show how many points the class will get each day. The first day has been done for you.

Part B In the last row of the table, write the total number of small cans and the total number of large cans. Figure out the total number of points for the whole week.

 If you have trouble with this problem, review the following lessons:
1.3, "The Meaning of Addition and Subtraction"
1.4, "Adding Whole Numbers"
1.6, "The Meaning of Multiplication"
1.7, "Multiplying Whole Numbers"

Unit 1

2. Mr. Motroni has 24 garden tiles that he wants to paint. He wants to paint one-half of the tiles blue, one-third of the tiles yellow, and one-sixth of them red. Figure out how many of each kind of tile Mr. Motroni will have. Fill in the table at the bottom with your answers.

Number of Blue Tiles	
Number of Yellow Tiles	
Number of Red Tiles	
Total Number of Tiles	

✔ If you have trouble with this problem, review the following lessons:
1.8, "The Meaning of Division"
1.11, "Fractions"

IDENTIFYING PATTERNS

This lesson addresses Benchmark MA.D.1.2.1 of the Sunshine State Standards.

The Challenge

Students at Fairview School are creating a garden. Each year, the classes plant another row of flowers. Look at the pattern of flowers. How many plants will the children add next year?

Learning the Ropes

A **pattern** can be made of shapes, numbers, or anything! The parts of the pattern either repeat or change. Each pattern has a **rule** that explains what happens to produce the next part of the pattern.

This letter pattern repeats:

A   B   C   A   B   C   A   ...

Can you tell what the next letter will be? The pattern repeats the letters A, B, C, so the next letter will be B.

This pattern of shapes repeats:

What shape will be next?

This number pattern follows a rule:

1   3   5   7   ...

Can you tell what the next number will be? The changes in this pattern follow the rule "add 2." To find the next number, you add 7 + 2 to get 9.

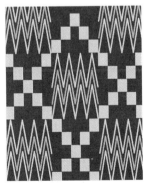

Math in Use: Early Learning Even babies know patterns! Scientists are studying how babies learn. A seven-month-old baby can respond to sounds in an A-B-A pattern. An A-B-A pattern repeats the same sound at the beginning and the end, like this: "li ti li, li ti li" and "wo fe wo, wo fe wo." A baby can tell the difference between the A-B-A pattern and an A-B-B pattern. An A-B-B pattern repeats the same sound at the end, like this: "li ti ti, li ti ti" or "wo fe fe, wo fe fe."

Rules for changes in patterns with numbers can use addition, subtraction, multiplication, or division. Here is an addition pattern:

> 1   4   7   10   …

The rule is "add 3." The next number in this pattern is 13 (10 + 3 = 13).

Here is a multiplication pattern:

> 1   3   9   27   …

The rule is "multiply by 3." The next number in this pattern is 81 (27 × 3 = 81).

Meeting the Challenge

To answer the Challenge, figure out if the pattern repeats or changes because of a rule. Count the number of plants in each row. Figure out what the rule for the pattern is. Then find the next row.

STEP 1: Count the plants in each row. The numbers are 1, 2, 4, 8, …. The pattern does not repeat, so it must change according to a rule.

STEP 2: What rule does this pattern follow? Each number is twice as big as the one before, so the rule is "multiply by 2."

STEP 3: To find the number of plants in the fifth row, multiply the number in the fourth row by 2. The number of plants in the fifth row will be 16 (8 × 2 = 16).

The answer to the Challenge is that the children will add 16 plants next year.

Try It Yourself

A. Fill in the circle next to the correct answer to each multiple-choice question.

1. What is the rule for this number pattern?

   52, 46, 40, 34, 28, …

   Ⓐ Divide by 6.

   Ⓑ Subtract 6.

   Ⓒ Subtract 4.

   Ⓓ Multiply by 4.

2. These triangles follow a pattern.

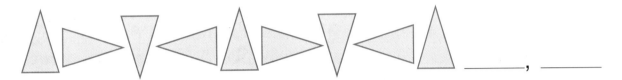

   Which triangles come next in the pattern?

   Ⓐ 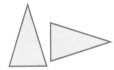   Ⓒ

   Ⓑ 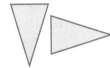   Ⓓ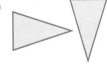

3. Which way does the next arrow in this pattern point?

   Ⓐ   Ⓑ   Ⓒ   Ⓓ

Go On

4. What is the next number in this pattern?

5, 10, 15, 20, 25, _____

Ⓐ 26   Ⓑ 28   Ⓒ 30   Ⓓ 32

5. Which rule can be used to make the following number pattern?

116, 105, 94, 83, …

Ⓐ Subtract 9.   Ⓑ Divide by 2.   Ⓒ Subtract 10.   Ⓓ Subtract 11.

6. What shape comes next in this pattern?

Ⓐ   Ⓑ   Ⓒ   Ⓓ

7. Linda and Casey started with 48 boxes of Girl Scout cookies. They went out together to sell cookies for four days. Each day, they sold 6 boxes. Which pattern tells the number of boxes that they had left each day?

Ⓐ 6, 12, 18, 24, …   Ⓒ 42, 34, 24, 12, …

Ⓑ 42, 36, 30, 24, …   Ⓓ 45, 42, 39, 36, …

8. Complete the two parts below.

Part A The pattern below starts with 1. The numbers in the bottom row show the differences between the numbers in the top row. Fill in the boxes to show the next three numbers in the top row. Fill in the ovals in the bottom row to show the differences between the numbers you added to the top row.

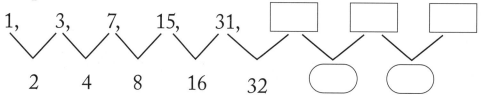

Part B What is the rule for this pattern? To go from one number to the next in the top row, you have to "multiply by 2 and _____."

PATTERNS WITH PAIRED NUMBERS

This lesson addresses Benchmarks MA.D.1.2.1 and MA.D.1.2.2 of the Sunshine State Standards.

Math in History

The words *money* and *mint* probably came from the name of an ancient Roman goddess. The Romans believed that the goddess Juno Moneta saved them from an attack in 390 B.C. They built a temple in her honor and later built a mint to make coins next to the temple. Coins and money often show us patterns with pairs of numbers, like $3 for 1 pen, $6 for 2 pens, $9 for 3 pens, and so on. What is the rule for this pattern?

The Challenge

A small box of crayons has 8 different-colored crayons in it. How many crayons will a classroom have if the teacher buys 7, 8, or 9 boxes? What is the pattern? Make a table to show the number of crayons for different numbers of boxes.

Learning the Ropes

Paired numbers are numbers that are related to each other according to a rule. A **table,** or **chart,** can help you see what the rule for a pattern is. The numbers in one row of a table are related to the numbers in the next row by a rule that explains the pattern for each pair. If you know the first number of a pair and the rule for what happens, then you also know what the second number will be.

EXAMPLE   A recipe says that one pot of soup will fill 4 bowls. How many bowls can you fill if you make 6 pots of soup? Notice the pattern in the table below.

Number of Pots of Soup	1	2	3	4	5	6
Number of Bowls Filled	4	8	12	16	20	?

One pot makes 4 bowls (1 × 4). Two pots make 8 bowls (2 × 4). The rule is "multiply by 4." To find the next number in the pattern, you must multiply 6 by 4: 6 × 4 = 24. The 6 pots of soup will fill 24 bowls.

Meeting the Challenge

To answer the Challenge, you must first find the rule for the pattern. When you know the rule, you can make a table that will show what happens in the pattern for these pairs of numbers.

STEP 1: Find the rule. Since 1 box has 8 crayons, 2 boxes will have 16 crayons (2 × 8). The rule is "multiply by 8."

STEP 2: Create a table. You do not have to use all the numbers between 1 and 9. Put the first number of the pair in the row labeled "Number of Boxes." Put the second number of the pair beneath it in the row labeled "Number of Crayons."

Number of Boxes	1	2	3	7	8	9
Number of Crayons	8	16	24	56	64	72

The answers to the Challenge are in the table. There will be 56 crayons in 7 boxes, 64 crayons in 8 boxes, and 72 crayons in 9 boxes.

Another Way Your table does not have to be horizontal (with rows going across). You can make vertical columns instead. The left column would show the number of boxes, and the right column would show the number of crayons.

Boxes	Crayons
1	8
2	16
3	24
7	56
8	64
9	72

Name _____ Class _____ Date _____

Try It Yourself

A. Fill in the circle next to the correct answer to each multiple-choice question.

1. Which rule does this table of numbers show?

1	2	3	4	5
4	6	8	10	12

- Ⓐ Multiply by 4.
- Ⓑ Multiply by 3, and then add 1.
- Ⓒ Multiply by 2, and then add 2.
- Ⓓ Add 3.

2. Which table shows the rule "add 2, and then multiply by 2"?

Ⓐ
1	2	3	4
2	4	6	8

Ⓒ
1	2	3	4
6	8	10	12

Ⓑ
1	2	3	4
2	3	4	5

Ⓓ
1	2	3	4
4	6	8	10

3. Which rule does this table of numbers show?

1	2	3	4	5
4	5	6	7	8

- Ⓐ Add 3.
- Ⓑ Add 1, and then multiply by 2.
- Ⓒ Multiply by 4.
- Ⓓ Multiply by 5, and then subtract 1.

Go On → **111**

4. If 1 ice cream cone costs $1.50 and 2 ice cream cones cost $3.00, how much will 3 ice cream cones cost?

Ⓐ $6.00   Ⓑ $4.50   Ⓒ $3.50   Ⓓ $3.00

B. Complete the four parts below. Show all your work.

The chart below shows the price of books at a used book sale. Use this chart to answer the questions in Parts A–D.

Number of Books	2	4	6	8
Cost in Dollars	$3	$6	$9	$12

Part A How much does one book cost?

Part B If Gerald has $10 to spend, how many books he can buy?

Part C How much will 10 books cost?

Part D Cynthia has saved $22. How much more does she need in order to buy 16 books?

CHANGE OVER TIME

This lesson addresses Benchmarks MA.D.1.2.1 and MA.D.1.2.2 of the Sunshine State Standards.

The Challenge

Every year on her birthday, Myame's mother measures her height. The chart to the right shows Myame's height at ages 5, 6, 7, and 8. How tall was she when she was 5 years old? How many inches did she grow between age 5 and age 8?

MYAME'S GROWTH	
Age (Years)	Height (Inches)
5	41
6	43
7	45
8	47

Math in History
For over 100 years, scientists have been studying tree rings. Counting the rings of a tree can tell you how old the tree is. Tree-ring counting has helped scientists to discover trees that are over 1,000 years old! Tree-ring counting can also tell you about how the weather changed from year to year. Wide rings mean more growth, in good weather; thin rings mean less growth, in bad weather.

Learning the Ropes

Everywhere you look, things change over time. Children grow taller. The temperature gets hotter or colder. The amount of money you have saved can get bigger or smaller.

You can keep track of changes in many ways. One way is to make a chart with paired numbers. In charts that show change over time, the first number is some measure of time, like seconds, minutes, hours, days, months or years. The second number is a measure of what is changing. This can be height, weight, or almost anything.

EXAMPLE The chart to the right shows how many dollars Karna has saved. On which day did he buy a book worth $5.00? On which day did he get $2.00 from his uncle?

KARNA'S SAVINGS	
Day	Money Saved
Monday	$12
Tuesday	$12
Wednesday	$ 7
Thursday	$ 7
Friday	$ 9

Look at the chart of Karna's savings on the previous page. The amount of money saved went from $12.00 on Tuesday to $7.00 on Wednesday. There was a change. On Wednesday, Karna had $5.00 less. This means that Karna bought his book on Wednesday. On Thursday, Karna still had $7.00, but on Friday there was another change. He now had $9.00. His uncle must have given him $2.00 on Friday.

Meeting the Challenge

To answer the Challenge, you must use the chart to see how Myame's height changed over time.

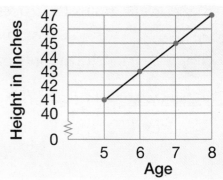

STEP 1: Use the chart to see how tall Myame was at age 5. The chart shows that at age 5, Myame was 41 inches tall.

STEP 2: Figure out how her height changed. Since Myame is growing each year, her height gets bigger. You can use subtraction to see how much she grows each year.

At age 6, she was 43 inches tall, and at age 5, she was 41 inches tall.
43 − 41 = 2 inches

At age 7, she was 45 inches tall, and at age 6, she was 43 inches tall.
45 − 43 = 2 inches

At age 8, she was 47 inches tall, and at age 7, she was 45 inches tall.
47 − 45 = 2 inches

Each year, she grew another two inches.

STEP 3: Subtract to figure out the total change. At age 8, she was 47 inches tall, and at age 5, she was 41 inches tall. She grew 6 inches (47 − 41 = 6).

The answer to the Challenge is that Myame was 41 inches tall at age 5. She grew 6 inches between age 5 and age 8.

Another Way Instead of using a chart, you could use a graph to show how height changes over time. The graph to the right shows Myame's height using a **line graph**.

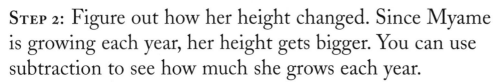
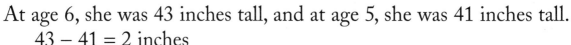

Name _____ Class _____ Date _____

Try It Yourself

A. Fill in the circle next to the correct answer to each multiple-choice question.

Use the chart to answer questions 1–4.

SCIENCE EXPERIMENT: HOW FAST DOES WATER COOL?	
Time	**Temperature**
Start	95°F
1 hour	90°F
2 hours	85°F
3 hours	75°F
4 hours	75°F

1. What happened to the temperature after 1 hour?
   Ⓐ It went up 5 degrees.
   Ⓑ It stayed the same.
   Ⓒ It went down 5 degrees.
   Ⓓ It went down 10 degrees.

2. What happened to the temperature between the first hour and the second hour?
   Ⓐ It went up 5 degrees.
   Ⓑ It stayed the same.
   Ⓒ It went down 5 degrees.
   Ⓓ It went down 10 degrees.

3. What happened to the temperature between the second hour and the third hour?
   Ⓐ It went up 5 degrees.
   Ⓑ It stayed the same.
   Ⓒ It went down 5 degrees.
   Ⓓ It went down 10 degrees.

4. After what hour did the temperature of the water stay the same?
   Ⓐ after 1 hour   Ⓑ after 2 hours   Ⓒ after 3 hours   Ⓓ after 4 hours

5. Which chart shows change over time?

Ⓐ

Boxes	Toys
1	3
2	6
3	9
4	12

Ⓒ

Week	Price
1	$10
2	$ 8
3	$ 7
4	$ 5

Ⓑ

Students	Pets
1	3
2	5
3	6
4	8

Ⓓ

Sides	Points
3	3
4	4
5	5
6	6

B. Complete the three parts below. Show all your work.

The chart to the right shows how much Ramon's weight has changed. Use this chart to answer the questions in Parts A–C.

RAMON'S WEIGHT	
Age (Years)	**Weight (Pounds)**
5	40
6	45
7	
8	
9	60

Part A How many pounds did Ramon gain between age 5 and age 6?

Part B What might Ramon's weight have been at age 7 and age 8? Fill in the blanks in the chart. Tell why you chose those numbers. (Hint: Use what you know about patterns from Lesson 2.2.)

Part C Make a guess at what Ramon's weight might be when he is 10 years old. Tell why you think your guess is a good one.

SOLVING NUMBER SENTENCES

This lesson addresses Benchmarks MA.D.2.2.1 and MA.D.2.2.2 of the Sunshine State Standards.

The Challenge

What numbers should go in the boxes in order to make each sentence true?

$$5 + \boxed{} = 20$$

$$5 \times \boxed{} = 20$$

Math in History
In our number system, we use written symbols like 1 and 987 to stand for numbers. About 500 years ago, the Incas of South America used knots in strings to represent numbers! With this number system, called *quipu*, the Incas could show place value and even solve number problems. Using the *quipu* as their basic number system, the Incas built a remarkable network of roads, farms, and businesses.

Learning the Ropes

A **number sentence** is a statement of something that is mathematically true. Each number sentence, or **equation,** contains an **equals sign** (=) and two or more numbers. It also has at least one **operation symbol,** like the plus sign: +. Here are some examples of number sentences:

$$1 + 2 = 3 \qquad 1 \times 2 \times 3 = 6 \qquad 3 - 1 = 2 \qquad 6 \div 3 = 2$$

When you **solve** a number sentence, you find the missing number that makes the sentence true. One way to solve number sentences is to think about fact families. **Fact families** are groups of number sentences that use the same numbers. The sentences are either about addition and subtraction or about multiplication and division.

EXAMPLE Here is an addition and subtraction fact family for the numbers 3, 4, and 7.

$$3 + 4 = 7 \qquad\qquad 4 + 3 = 7$$

$$7 - 3 = 4 \qquad\qquad 7 - 4 = 3$$

In the fact family on the previous page, the biggest number is 7. The other two numbers can be added together to make 7. When one number is subtracted from 7, you get the other.

EXAMPLE Here is a multiplication and division fact family for the numbers 3, 4, and 12:

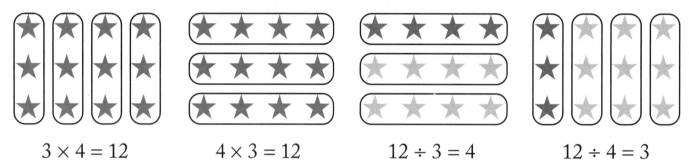

$$3 \times 4 = 12 \qquad 4 \times 3 = 12 \qquad 12 \div 3 = 4 \qquad 12 \div 4 = 3$$

In this fact family, the biggest number is 12. The other two numbers, when multiplied, make 12. When one number is divided into 12, you get the other.

Meeting the Challenge

To meet the Challenge, you must solve each problem using what you know about fact families.

STEP 1: Find the number that should go in the box in order to make the first number sentence true: $5 + \square = 20$. Since $5 + 15 = 20$, the missing number is 15. You can check your answer by thinking about the fact family and seeing that these numbers work:

$$5 + 15 = 20 \qquad 20 - 5 = 15$$
$$15 + 5 = 20 \qquad 20 - 15 = 5$$

STEP 2: Solve the second number sentence: $5 \times \square = 20$. Since $5 \times 4 = 20$, the missing number is 4. You can check your answer by thinking about the fact family and seeing that these numbers work:

$$5 \times 4 = 20 \qquad 20 \div 4 = 5$$
$$4 \times 5 = 20 \qquad 20 \div 5 = 4$$

Name _____ Class _____ Date _____

Try It Yourself

A. Fill in the circle next to the correct answer to each multiple-choice question.

1. What mathematical fact does this picture show?

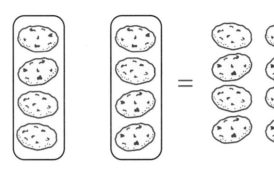

   Ⓐ $8 \div 2 = 4$ Ⓒ $6 + 2 = 8$

   Ⓑ $8 - 4 = 4$ Ⓓ $4 \times 2 = 8$

2. What number should go in the box in order to make this number sentence true? $(4 \times \boxed{}) + 5 = 16 + 5$

   Ⓐ 1   Ⓑ 2   Ⓒ 3   Ⓓ 4

3. What missing numbers will make these number sentences true?

   $8 - \boxed{} = 2, \qquad 8 \div \boxed{} = 2$

   Ⓐ 6 and 4   Ⓑ 4 and 4   Ⓒ 4 and 2   Ⓓ 2 and 2

4. What number should go in the box in order to make this number sentence true? $(20 + 4) + \boxed{} = 24 + 8$

   Ⓐ 3   Ⓑ 8   Ⓒ 21   Ⓓ 24

5. $3 \times 118 = 354$. What does $(3 \times 118) + 5$ equal?

   Ⓐ 123   Ⓑ 126   Ⓒ 359   Ⓓ 854

Go On

6. Ian and Joel both have some crayons. Ian has 21 crayons. Together, they have 32 crayons. Which number sentence can be solved to show how many crayons Joel has?

Ⓐ $21 + \boxed{} = 32$

Ⓑ $21 + 32 = \boxed{}$

Ⓒ $\boxed{} = 21 + 32$

Ⓓ $\boxed{} + 32 = 21$

7. What number should be put in both boxes in order to make the following number sentence true? (Hint: Try each answer to see if it works.)

$3 \times \boxed{} = (2 \times 4) + \boxed{}$

Ⓐ 1   Ⓑ 2   Ⓒ 3   Ⓓ 4

8. Complete the activity below.

The stars below represent a fact family. There are two multiplication facts and two division facts in the family. Write the whole fact family on the lines provided below.

★ ★ ★ ★ ★ ★
★ ★ ★ ★ ★ ★
★ ★ ★ ★ ★ ★

_____ × _____ = _____

_____ × _____ = _____

_____ ÷ _____ = _____

_____ ÷ _____ = _____

1. Mary Beth and Allison are playing a computer game. When they type in a number, the computer prints out another number. The game is to figure out what rule the computer uses. To help them solve the puzzle, they decide to make a table of what happens.

Number they type in	1	2	4	5	6
Number computer prints out	4	7	13	16	19

Part A What rule does the computer use?
(Hint: The rule uses both multiplication and addition.)

Part B If the girls type in the number 3, what number will the computer print out?

✔ If you have trouble with this problem, review the following lessons:
    2.1, "Identifying Patterns"
    2.2, "Patterns with Paired Numbers"

Unit 2

2. During rainy weeks, Samantha likes to measure how deep a puddle near her house is. Every evening, she goes out and measures the puddle's depth. Before Sunday, there was no puddle at all. Here is a table of her measurements for one week.

Day	Puddle Depth
Sunday	3 inches
Monday	7 inches
Tuesday	8 inches
Wednesday	10 inches
Thursday	9 inches
Friday	5 inches
Saturday	6 inches

Use the information in the table to answer the following questions. Show all your work.

Part A On which days did rain fall?

Part B On which day did the most rain fall?

Part C On which days did the depth of the puddle go down?

✔ If you have trouble with this problem, review the following lessons:
2.3, "Change over Time"
2.4, "Solving Number Sentences"

BASIC GEOMETRIC FIGURES

This lesson addresses Benchmarks MA.B.1.2.1, MA.B.1.2.2, and MA.C.1.2.1 of the Sunshine State Standards.

Math in History

"String art" was a popular way to make designs and pictures in the 1970s. You can make a picture by winding string around nails, as shown below. Each nail is a point. You can use string to connect the points, just as you can connect dots to make shapes. Think of the string between two points as a line segment. Angles are formed when two line segments cross each other. Other angles are formed when the string extends in two different directions from the same point.

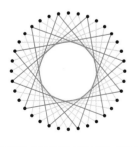

The Challenge

Look at the map. Stop signs need to be put at corners where the streets are perpendicular to each other. Stop lights need to be put at corners where the streets form an acute angle. Which corners need stop signs? Which corners need stop lights?

Learning the Ropes

The chart below lists several terms used to describe a line and its parts.

•	•——•	•——→	←——→
point	**line segment**	**ray**	**line**

A **point** is a single spot in space. A **line segment** connects two points—the **endpoints** of the segment. A **ray** has one endpoint and goes on forever in one direction. All of these are parts of a **line,** which goes on forever in both directions.

When two rays begin at the same endpoint, they form an **angle.** The endpoint they share is called the **vertex** of the angle. The chart on the next page shows four kinds of angles.

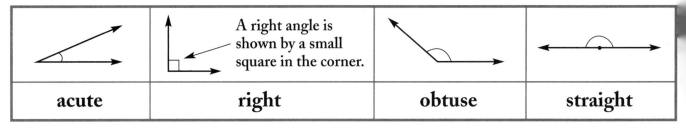

acute	right	obtuse	straight

Angles are measured by the space between the rays that form them. An angle is measured in **degrees**. An **acute angle** measures less than 90 degrees (90°). A **right angle** measures exactly 90°. An **obtuse angle** measures more than 90°. A **straight angle** measures 180 degrees (180°). It looks like a straight line.

Here are some ways that two lines can be related to each other:

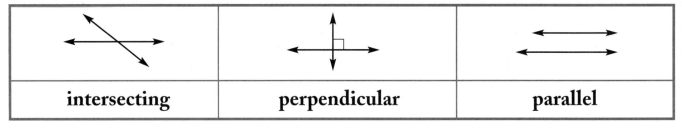

intersecting	perpendicular	parallel

When two lines cross, they are said to **intersect**. Two lines that form a right angle when they cross are called **perpendicular lines.** Two lines that are side by side but never meet or cross are called **parallel lines.**

Meeting the Challenge

To answer the Challenge, find two different kinds of angles on the map.

STEP 1: Look for perpendicular lines. They form right angles where Pine Street meets Main Street and where Oak Street meets Main Street.

STEP 2: Look for acute angles. Hill Street makes an acute angle with Main Street.

The answer to the Challenge is that one stop sign is needed at the corner where Oak Street meets Main Street and another stop sign is needed where Main Street meets Pine Street. A stop light is needed at Main and Hill Street.

Another Way Compare the square corner of a sheet of paper with the angles formed by the streets on the map. If the angles are the same, then the streets are at right angles to each other.

Name _____ Class _____ Date _____

Try It Yourself

A. Fill in the circle next to the correct answer to each multiple-choice question.

1. You are flying a kite. The string is stretched out straight from your hand to the kite. What term best describes the string between your hand and the kite?

   Ⓐ point

   Ⓑ line segment

   Ⓒ ray

   Ⓓ right angle

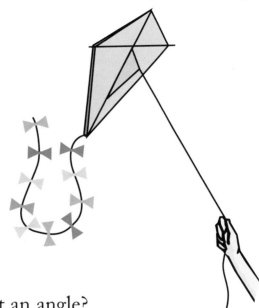

2. Which statement is NOT true about an angle?

   Ⓐ An angle can be formed by intersecting lines.

   Ⓑ Two rays that meet at an endpoint form an angle.

   Ⓒ An angle has two vertices.

   Ⓓ An angle is measured by the size of the opening between its rays.

3. The blades of this opened pair of scissors form what kind of angle?

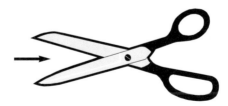

   Ⓐ 90°   Ⓑ obtuse   Ⓒ acute   Ⓓ right

4. Intersecting lines can form all of the following EXCEPT

   Ⓐ right angles.   Ⓒ obtuse angles.

   Ⓑ acute angles.   Ⓓ parallel lines.

Go On ⟩

5. Which type of angle measures more than 90°?

   Ⓐ acute angle   Ⓒ obtuse angle

   Ⓑ right angle   Ⓓ 30° angle

6. Which of the following are parallel?

   Ⓐ the hands on a clock

   Ⓑ the top and left side of a sheet of paper

   Ⓒ the lines that make the capital letter L

   Ⓓ the left and right edges of a door

B. Complete the two parts below.

Think about the angles formed by the two hands of a clock.

Part A What kind of angle is formed by the hands of this clock?

Part B

• Name a time when the hands of a clock would make a right angle. Draw the hands on the first clock below.

• Name a time when the hands would make a straight line. Draw the hands on the middle clock below.

• Name a time when the hands would make an acute angle. Draw them on the third clock below.

Right angle

Time: _____

Straight angle

Time: _____

Acute angle

Time: _____

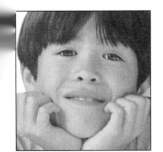

TWO-DIMENSIONAL SHAPES

This lesson addresses Benchmark MA.C.1.2.1 of the Sunshine State Standards.

The Challenge

The map to the right shows some pieces of land along High View Road. Which pieces of land are quadrilaterals?

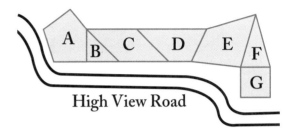

High View Road

Learning the Ropes

The table below tells about some basic flat shapes. A flat shape has **two dimensions**—length and width.

Shape	Definition
circle diameter	A **circle** is made up of points that are all the same distance from its **center**—the point in the middle. The **diameter**—the distance across a circle through the center—is always the same length.
triangle	A **triangle** is a shape that has three sides and three angles.
quadrilateral	A **quadrilateral** is a shape that has four sides and four angles.

Math in History

Most houses are built in the shape of a rectangle or a square. If you go to the Old Naval Yard of the Pensacola Naval Air Station, however, you will see a house built in the shape of an **octagon** (eight-sided figure). The octagon house, called simply Building 16, was constructed in 1834. Many octagon houses were built in the middle of the nineteenth century. These houses were said to have more space than other houses. They were also said to be more healthful because they could have window openings on all eight sides.

A **polygon** is a closed shape with straight sides. Triangles and quadrilaterals are polygons. The shapes shown below are special triangles and quadrilaterals.

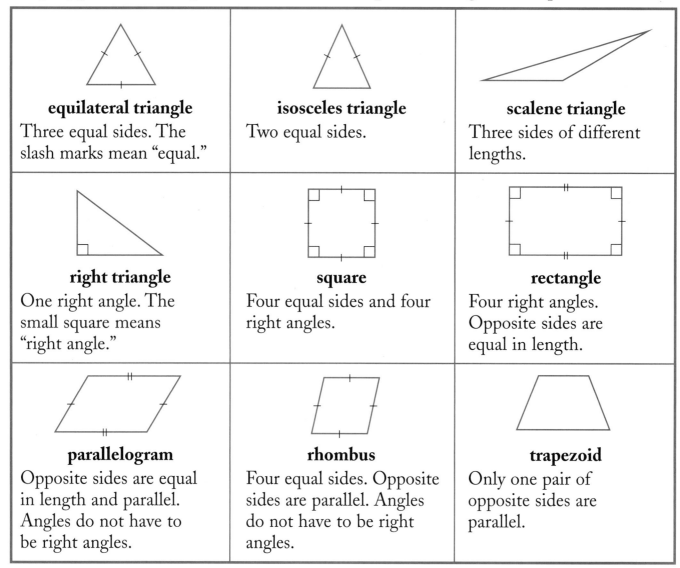

equilateral triangle
Three equal sides. The slash marks mean "equal."

isosceles triangle
Two equal sides.

scalene triangle
Three sides of different lengths.

right triangle
One right angle. The small square means "right angle."

square
Four equal sides and four right angles.

rectangle
Four right angles. Opposite sides are equal in length.

parallelogram
Opposite sides are equal in length and parallel. Angles do not have to be right angles.

rhombus
Four equal sides. Opposite sides are parallel. Angles do not have to be right angles.

trapezoid
Only one pair of opposite sides are parallel.

Meeting the Challenge

To answer the Challenge, you need to look at the shapes of the pieces of land to see which ones are quadrilaterals.

Look for four-sided figures. If you said C, D, E, and G, you are correct!

Another Way To answer the Challenge, you can look at the shapes to see which ones have too few sides or too many. Start with the three-sided shapes and cross them out. Next, cross out figures with more than four sides. The four shapes that are left all have four sides. They are all quadrilaterals.

Name _____ Class _____ Date _____

Try It Yourself

A. Fill in the circle next to the correct answer to each multiple-choice question.

1. A right triangle has how many right angles?
   Ⓐ four   Ⓑ three   Ⓒ two   Ⓓ one

2. What do an equilateral triangle and a square have in common?
   Ⓐ They both have at least one right angle.
   Ⓑ All sides are equal in length.
   Ⓒ All angles are acute angles.
   Ⓓ They are both quadrilaterals.

3. What do a rhombus and a parallelogram have in common?
   Ⓐ They both have four equal sides.
   Ⓑ They both have four equal angles.
   Ⓒ They both have at least one right angle.
   Ⓓ They both have two pairs of opposite sides that are parallel.

4. Which of the following is a polygon?

   Ⓐ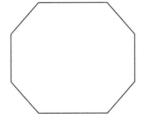

   Ⓒ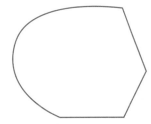

   Ⓑ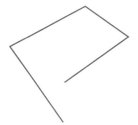

   Ⓓ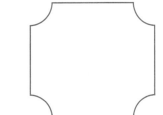

Go On

5. What do a rhombus and a square have in common?

  Ⓐ They both have four equal sides.

  Ⓑ They both have four equal angles.

  Ⓒ They both have at least one right angle.

  Ⓓ They both have only one pair of opposite sides that are parallel.

6. Which of these shapes has no parallel sides?

  Ⓐ rectangle   Ⓒ triangle

  Ⓑ parallelogram   Ⓓ trapezoid

7. If you cut a square in half **diagonally** (from corner to corner), what shapes do you get?

  Ⓐ two isosceles triangles

  Ⓑ two squares

  Ⓒ two trapezoids

  Ⓓ two scalene triangles

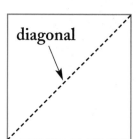

8. Complete the four parts below.

The figure to the right is an equilateral triangle divided up into some smaller shapes. Use the figure to answer Parts A–D.

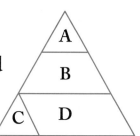

Part A What kind of figure is shape D?

Part B Name two shapes that together form a trapezoid.

Part C If you cut triangle A off the top of the figure, what figure is left?

Part D What kind of figure is formed by shapes A, B, and D together? (Hint: It might help to look at the figure sideways.)

THREE-DIMENSIONAL SHAPES

This lesson addresses Benchmark MA.C.1.2.1 of the Sunshine State Standards.

The Challenge

Your little sister has a set of wooden blocks with all the shapes shown in the picture. Which shapes could you stack up? Explain your answers.

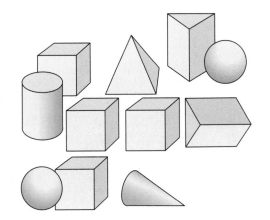

Math in History
Serenus was a mathematician born in Egypt around A.D. 300. He was interested in the two-dimensional shapes that you get when you slice through three-dimensional shapes. Suppose you cut an orange through the middle. The flat part of each half is a circle. You can also get circles by cutting through a cone.

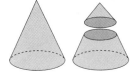

Learning the Ropes

Circles and polygons are flat. They have two dimensions—length and width. They have no height (thickness).

Solid shapes have **three dimensions**—length, width, and height. For example, a box of cereal can be about 8 inches long and 10 inches high. It can also be about 2 inches wide (thick). The chart below shows some three-dimensional shapes.

sphere	cube	cylinder	cone
![sphere]	![cube]	![cylinder]	![cone]
rectangular prism	**triangular prism**	**square pyramid**	**triangular pyramid**
![rectangular prism]	![triangular prism]	![square pyramid]	![triangular pyramid]

Unit 3: Geometry and Spatial Sense   **131**

Math in Use: Baseballs Did you ever wonder what a baseball is made of? The innermost part of the ball is a small sphere. It is about the size of a grape. It is made of cork. The cork center is covered with rubber. Cotton and wool yarn are wound tightly around the cork and rubber center. Then, the ball is covered with two pieces of leather and sewn together. Before 1848, baseballs had a solid rubber core. They were smaller and livelier, which means that they could bounce higher and go farther. With those lively balls, teams could score over a hundred runs!

The flat sides of three-dimensional shapes are called **faces.** The face that a shape sits on is its **base.** A cone has one flat face. A cylinder has two flat faces. A cube has six flat faces. How many faces does a rectangular prism have? How many faces does a triangular prism have? How about a square pyramid? A triangular pyramid? Does a sphere have any faces?

Meeting the Challenge

To answer the Challenge, you need to look at the different shapes and see if they have any flat sides (faces). Think about how the shapes might be stacked.

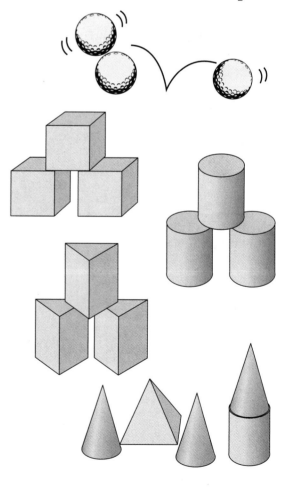

STEP 1: Ask yourself if spheres can be stacked. The answer is "no." Spheres have no faces, so there is no flat side to rest on. Imagine trying to stack a dozen golf balls!

STEP 2: Cubes (which are special rectangular prisms) have flat sides, or faces. It is easy to stack them on top of each other.

STEP 3: Cylinders can be stacked if the flat faces are on the top and bottom.

STEP 4: If you turn triangular prisms so that the triangular faces are on the top and bottom, they can be stacked.

STEP 5: Cones and pyramids cannot be stacked on top of each other. You could put one cone or pyramid on top of a figure with a flat top.

Name _____ Class _____ Date _____

Try It Yourself

A. Fill in the circle next to the correct answer to each multiple-choice question.

1. What is the name for this shape?

   Ⓐ cube

   Ⓑ square pyramid

   Ⓒ rectangular pyramid

   Ⓓ rectangular prism

   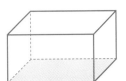

2. Look at the items on the "Garage Sale" sign. Which object looks most like a cylinder?

   Ⓐ toaster   Ⓑ coffee pot   Ⓒ lampshade   Ⓓ puzzle

3. Which of the following shapes is a prism?

Go On ⇒

4. What is the name for this shape?

Ⓐ cone

Ⓑ triangular pyramid

Ⓒ square pyramid

Ⓓ triangular prism

5. Which of the following objects is NOT a cylinder?

Ⓐ

Ⓒ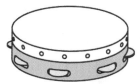

Ⓑ

Ⓓ

6. Which of the following shapes has six faces?

Ⓐ

Ⓒ

Ⓑ

Ⓓ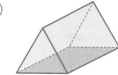

8. Complete the three parts below. Use your own paper.

Think about the following shapes and their names. Use these names to answer the three questions about shapes below.

| cone | cube | sphere | cylinder | square pyramid | rectangular prism |

Part A Which three shapes would you be able to roll most easily?

Part B Which three shapes could you stand on most easily?

Part C Which shape has exactly one point, or **vertex**?

CONGRUENT SHAPES

This lesson addresses Benchmarks MA.C.2.2.1 of the Sunshine State Standards.

The Challenge

A children's book company was making books in unusual shapes and sizes. One day, the pages from different books were mixed up by mistake. Look at the pages below. Which pages belong together?

Math in History
Origami, the Japanese art of paper-folding, began in ancient times. Specially folded paper was used for certificates in important ceremonies. Later, people used origami as a way to wrap letters and decorate presents. Masters of origami create interesting shapes. What congruent figures do you see in the origami below?

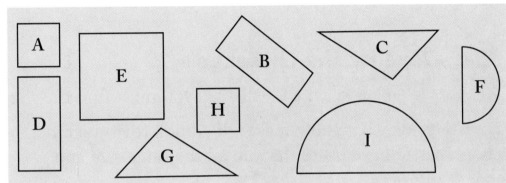

Learning the Ropes

Figures that are the same size and shape are called **congruent.** If you put one congruent shape on top of the other, the shapes will match exactly.

EXAMPLES

These triangles are congruent.

These quadrilaterals are congruent.

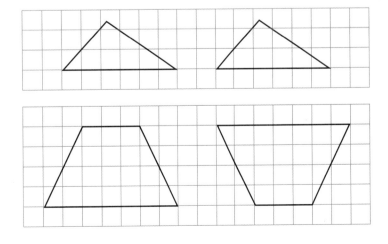

Math in Use: Art Andy Warhol, a famous artist, created some unusual artwork by using congruent shapes. He repeated a picture of an object or a face over and over. One of his paintings has 32 identical images of a soup can.

These triangles are *not* congruent.

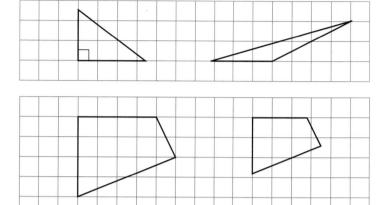

These quadrilaterals are *not* congruent.

Meeting the Challenge

To answer the Challenge, you must find the shapes that match.

STEP 1: Decide what allows pages of a book to go together. A book has to have pages that are all the same size and shape (congruent).

STEP 2: Look for figures that are the same shape. Figures A, E, and H are all squares. Figures B and D are rectangles. Figures C and G are both triangles. Figures F and I are both half-circles.

STEP 3: If the shapes are the same, see if their sizes match. A and H are squares that are the same size and shape, so they are congruent. E is a square, too, but it is larger than A and H. Rectangle B is tilted, but it is the same size and shape as D, so shapes B and D are also congruent. Triangles C and G are the same shape and size, so they are congruent. Figures F and I are the same shape but are different sizes, so they are not congruent.

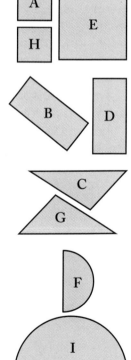

The answer to the Challenge is that pages A and H are congruent, so they can go together in the same book. Pages B and D belong together in another book. Congruent pages C and G belong together in a third book.

Try It Yourself

3.4 Congruent Shapes

A. Fill in the circle next to the correct answer to each multiple-choice question.

1. Which shapes are congruent?

Ⓐ 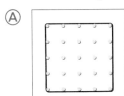 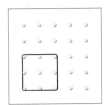   Ⓒ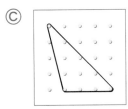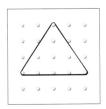

Ⓑ 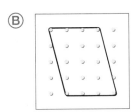 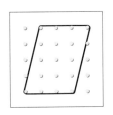   Ⓓ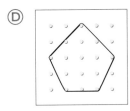

2. The stars in this quilt pattern need to be the same size and shape. Which star goes in the white spaces?

Ⓐ   Ⓑ   Ⓒ    Ⓓ

3. Which shapes are congruent?

Ⓐ    Ⓒ

Ⓑ   Ⓓ

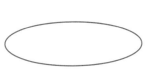 **137**

4. Which of the following shapes is NOT congruent to this quadrilateral? ⟶

Ⓐ

Ⓒ

Ⓑ

Ⓓ

5. Which of the following statements is true?
   Ⓐ All equilateral triangles are congruent.
   Ⓑ All right triangles are congruent.
   Ⓒ All squares are congruent.
   Ⓓ All circles with the same diameter are congruent.

B. Complete the activity below.

When you do a jigsaw puzzle, you have to find a piece that is congruent to (matches) each hole in the puzzle. Finish this puzzle by telling which piece goes in each hole. The first one is done for you. Remember that you may have to turn the pieces to make them fit.

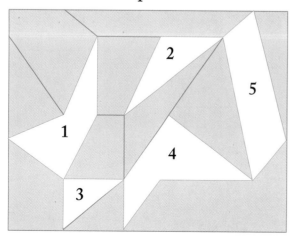

1. __E__
2. ____
3. ____
4. ____
5. ____

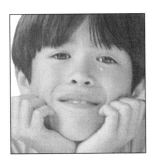

SYMMETRY

This lesson addresses Benchmark MA.C.2.2.1 of the Sunshine State Standards.

The Challenge

Mrs. Bailey showed her class some flag designs. She asked them whether or not the designs were symmetrical. Which ones are symmetrical? Where are the lines of symmetry?

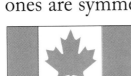

Canada   Jamaica   Red Cross    United States

Learning the Ropes

A shape shows **symmetry** if it can be divided into two matching or congruent halves. The line that divides the shape into two congruent halves is called the **line of symmetry**.

Look at the shapes in the chart below. Can you tell what makes them symmetrical or not?

Symmetrical	Not Symmetrical

Math in History

Oriental rugs are well known for their beautiful patterns. Many of the patterns on the rugs show symmetry. Look at the design below, which is similar to part of a small nineteenth-century rug from Turkey. The star shown in the design is symmetrical. How many lines of symmetry can you identify in the star from this rug?

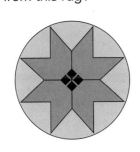

Shapes can have one, two, or many lines of symmetry. How many lines of symmetry does the shape of a stop sign have? It has 8 lines of symmetry, as shown to the right.

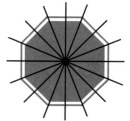

A circle has an infinite number of lines of symmetry—too many to count. Every diameter (line through the center) is a line of symmetry.

Meeting the Challenge

To answer the Challenge, you must figure out whether or not the designs are symmetrical. Then show where the lines of symmetry are.

STEP 1: The flag of Canada has one line of symmetry. The left half is a mirror image of the right half.

STEP 2: The flag of Jamaica has two lines of symmetry.

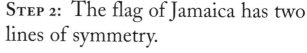

STEP 3: The symbol of the Red Cross has four lines of symmetry.

STEP 4: The flag of the United States is not symmetrical.

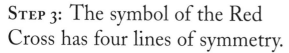

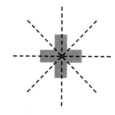

Another Way You can use a mirror to check whether or not a design is symmetrical. Fold the design in half. Hold it up to a mirror. If you see the whole design, then the fold is a line of symmetry. What you see in the mirror is the **mirror image,** or **reflection,** of what you hold up to the mirror.

Try It Yourself

A. Fill in the circle next to the correct answer to each multiple-choice question.

1. Which of the following figures is symmetrical?

   Ⓐ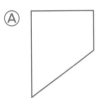

   Ⓒ

   Ⓑ

   Ⓓ

2. The thick lines below form half of a letter. The other half is missing. The dotted line is a line of symmetry of the letter. What is the letter?

   Ⓐ **N**   Ⓑ **W**   Ⓒ **V**   Ⓓ **M**

3. Which of these pictures shows a line of symmetry?

   Ⓐ

   Ⓒ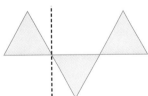

   Ⓑ

   Ⓓ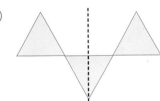

Go On 141

4. Which of the following figures is symmetrical?

Ⓐ

Ⓒ

Ⓑ

Ⓓ

5. How many lines of symmetry does this figure have?

Ⓐ none   Ⓒ 4

Ⓑ 1   Ⓓ 6

6. Which capital letter below has exactly two lines of symmetry?

Ⓐ **T**   Ⓑ **E**   Ⓒ **H**   Ⓓ **Z**

7. Complete the activity below.

These shapes are used for road signs. Draw all the lines of symmetry for each shape.

 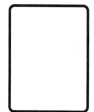  

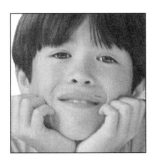

PLOTTING POINTS

This lesson addresses Benchmark MA.C.3.2.2 of the Sunshine State Standards.

Math in History

Heijo-kyo was a Japanese city built more than 1,200 years ago. It was laid out on a grid pattern, with straight streets running north and south or east and west. The city was big—almost 10 square miles. The grid pattern made it easier for people to find their way around the city without getting lost.

The Challenge

Look at the grid. Each vertical line is a street running north-south. Each horizontal line is a street running east-west. Mrs. Carlson is at the traffic light at point *A*. There is another traffic light at point *B*. Mrs. Carlson wants to go to the bakery at the second traffic light. How many blocks east should she go? How many blocks north?

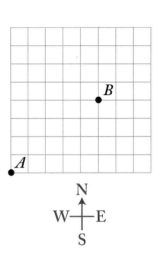

Learning the Ropes

A **coordinate grid** is made up of evenly spaced lines. The lines are **horizontal** (left-right) and **vertical** (up-down). A **point** on a grid is the place where a horizontal line intersects a vertical line. In the picture below, *A*, *B*, and *C* are three points on the grid.

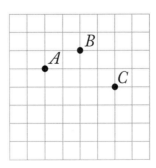

One way to identify points on a grid is to give each line a number. Start at the left, with zero. Moving to the right, label each vertical line with a number.

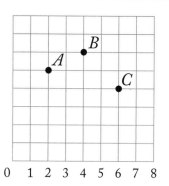

To label the horizontal lines, start at the bottom, with zero. Label each horizontal line with a number as you move up from zero.

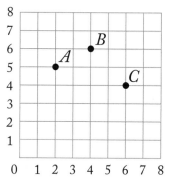

Each point now has a pair of numbers, or **coordinates**—one from its vertical line and one from its horizontal line. Point *A* is on vertical line 2 and horizontal line 5. The location for a point is usually written like this: *A*(2, 5). Point *B* is located at *B*(4, 6). Where is point *C* located? If you said point *C* is located at *C*(6, 4), you would be correct! Notice that points *B* and *C* use the same numbers (4 and 6) but in a different order. When you **plot** (mark) points, always go right first and then up.

Meeting the Challenge

To answer the Challenge, number the streets on the grid. Then find the bakery's location.

STEP 1: Number the streets on the grid.

STEP 2: Locate the bakery. It is located at *B*(5, 4). Mrs. Carlson should go 5 blocks east and then 4 blocks north.

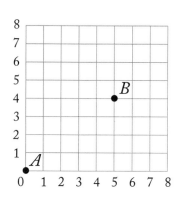

Name _____ Class _____ Date _____

Try It Yourself

A. Fill in the circle next to the correct answer to each multiple-choice question.

Use the grid below to answer questions 1–6.

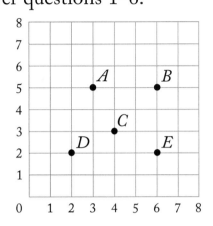

1. What point is at $(3, 5)$?

    Ⓐ A Ⓑ B Ⓒ C Ⓓ D

2. What point is at $(2, 2)$?

    Ⓐ A Ⓑ B Ⓒ C Ⓓ D

3. What point is at $(6, 5)$?

    Ⓐ A Ⓑ B Ⓒ C Ⓓ D

4. What is the location of point E?

    Ⓐ $E(2, 2)$ Ⓑ $E(2, 6)$ Ⓒ $E(6, 2)$ Ⓓ $E(6, 6)$

5. How far is it from point D to point E?

    Ⓐ 2 spaces   Ⓑ 4 spaces   Ⓒ 6 spaces   Ⓓ 8 spaces

6. If you move right from point C and then up to point B, how many spaces do you move?

    Ⓐ 2 spaces   Ⓑ 3 spaces   Ⓒ 4 spaces   Ⓓ 8 spaces

Go On

7. Suppose you have a grid that goes across 10 and up 10. How would you go from point (5, 10) to point (10, 5)?

Ⓐ Go to the right and up.

Ⓑ Go to the right and down.

Ⓒ Go to the left and up.

Ⓓ Go to the left and down.

8. Complete the four parts below.

As you answer the questions below, use this grid to plot (mark) points.

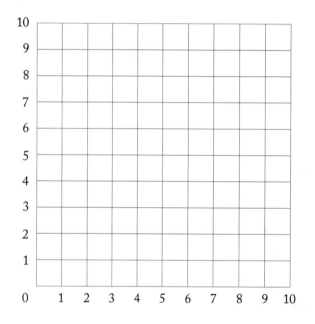

Part A Point *Q* is at (1, 2). Point *R* is at (3, 4). Point *S* is at (8, 4). Mark these three points on the grid.

Part B Points *Q, R,* and *S* are three corners of a parallelogram. Find and label point *T,* the other corner of the parallelogram.

Part C Mark point *J* at (2, 6). Mark point *K* at (6, 6). Mark one more point *L* that will form an isosceles triangles with points *J* and *K.* (There are many different answers.)

Part D Mark points *M*(7, 7) and *N*(8, 8). Name another point *P* that will be on the same line as these two points.

TRANSFORMING SHAPES

This lesson addresses Benchmarks MA.C.2.2.1 and MA.C.2.2.2 of the Sunshine State Standards.

The Challenge

Shape A has been transformed into Shape B. What two transformations were done to change A into B?

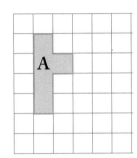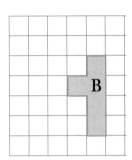

Math in History

In 1884, LaMarcus Thompson built the first roller coaster in the United States. It was a ride at Coney Island in Brooklyn, New York. It was called the Gravity Pleasure Switchback Railway. It takes a lot of mathematics to build a roller coaster!

Learning the Ropes

A **transformation** moves an object around but doesn't change the shape. One kind of transformation is called a slide. A **slide** just moves the object from one place to another. In the picture below, the shape slides to the right.

Another kind of transformation is called a turn. A **turn** spins, or **rotates,** the object around a point. In the first picture below, the shape turns around a point outside the shape. In the next picture, the shape turns around a point inside the shape.

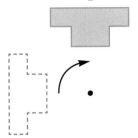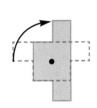

A third kind of transformation is called a flip. A **flip** turns a shape over a line. The result looks like a mirror image of the first shape. In the picture to the right, the shape has been flipped over the dotted line. The "E" shape now looks like a "Ǝ" shape. If you look at the "E" shape in a mirror, it will look like the "Ǝ" shape.

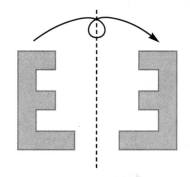

Meeting the Challenge

To answer the Challenge, you must use what you know about transformations.

STEP 1: Ask yourself, "What happened to the shape?" Shape B is a mirror image of Shape A. First, you need to flip the shape. (Figure 1)

STEP 2: Again ask yourself, "What happened?" The shape is still too high. Slide it down. (Figure 2)

The answer to the Challenge is that the shape had two transformations. The first was a flip, and the second was a slide.

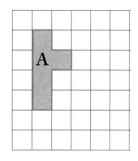
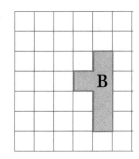

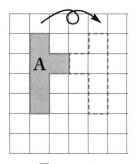
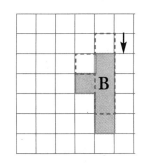

Figure 1   Figure 2

Another Way To see how shapes can translate, try drawing a shape on paper and cutting it out. Then you can slide, flip, and rotate the shape on your own.

Try It Yourself

3.7 Transforming Shapes

A. Fill in the circle next to the correct answer to each multiple-choice question.

1. Which picture shows a slide transformation?

Ⓐ 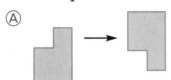 Ⓒ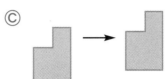

Ⓑ 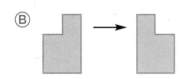 Ⓓ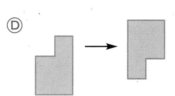

2. Which triangle shows a turn of the shaded triangle?
   Ⓐ Triangle A
   Ⓑ Triangle B
   Ⓒ Triangle C
   Ⓓ Triangle D

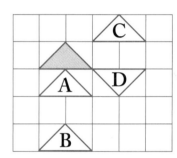

3. Which shape below is a flip of this shape?

Ⓐ  Ⓑ  Ⓒ  Ⓓ

4. Which amusement park attraction has flips in it?
   Ⓐ roller coaster   Ⓒ merry-go-round
   Ⓑ hall of mirrors   Ⓓ Ferris wheel

Go On 149

5. A square has been cut into four shapes. What transformation do the four shapes show?

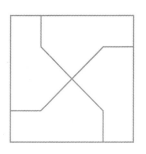

Ⓐ turn

Ⓑ flip

Ⓒ slide

Ⓓ diameter

B. Complete the two parts below.

Transformations of a shape that can fill all the space are called **tessellations.** Here are three examples:

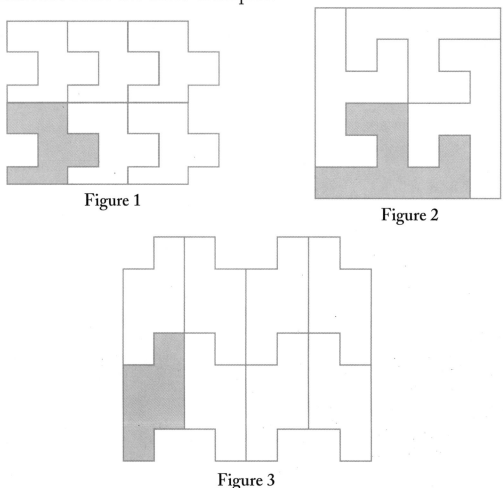

Figure 1

Figure 2

Figure 3

Part A Look at the three tessellations above. Which tessellation has just slides in it? Which tessellation has flips in it? Which tessellation has rotations (turns) in it?

Part B On your own paper, draw some tessellations of your own.

UNIT 3 EXTRA CHALLENGE

1. Kyle drew the six shapes below. He wants to arrange them into three groups (pairs). There will be two shapes in each pair.

Unit 3

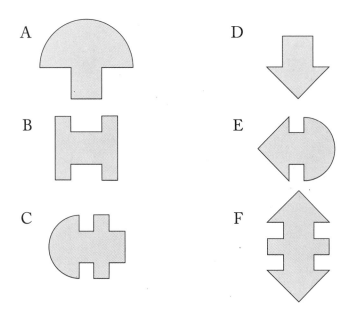

Think about how many lines of symmetry each shape has. Notice what direction the lines go. Tell Kyle what pairs of shapes go together.

Explain why you chose the pairs you did.

✔ If you have trouble with this problem, review the following lessons:
3.4, "Congruent Shapes"
3.5, "Symmetry"

2. The grid below shows two points, *A* and *C*. Point *A* is at (3, 2). Point *C* is at (6, 5).

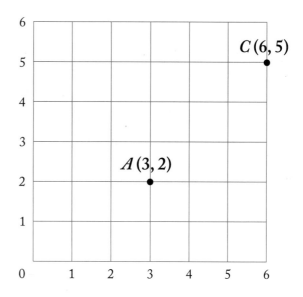

Find two more points, *B* and *D*, that can make the square *ABCD*. Mark and label the two points.

Explain how you found your answer.

✔ If you have trouble with this problem, review the following lessons:
3.1, "Basic Geometric Figures"
3.2, "Two-Dimensional Shapes"
3.6, "Plotting Points"

MEASURING LENGTH: CUSTOMARY UNITS

This lesson addresses Benchmarks MA.B.1.2.1, MA.B.1.2.2, MA.B.2.2.1, MA.B.2.2.2, MA.B.3.2.1, MA.B.4.2.1, and MA.B.4.2.2 of the Sunshine State Standards.

The Challenge

Connie is writing with a pencil. Is the pencil about 5 feet long, 5 yards long, or 5 inches long?

Learning the Ropes

Math in History
Thousands of years ago in Europe, Romans made arch bridges out of stone. More recently stone arch bridges were also made in the United States. Some of these are still standing today. The Stone Arch Bridge in Minnesota is 2,100 feet long and 76 feet high. Most arch bridges today are made from concrete or steel.

In the United States, **customary units,** like inches, miles, pounds, and quarts are used to **measure,** or tell how big something is. Look at the chart below.

Customary Unit	Objects for Comparing	Number Sentences
inch (in.)	a small paper clip	12 in. = 1 ft 36 in. = 1 yd
foot (ft)	the length of a football	1 ft = 12 in. 3 ft = 1 yd
yard (yd)	the width of a doorway	1 yd = 3 ft 1 yd = 36 in.

Often you can **estimate,** or guess, how long something is by comparing it to something you know.

EXAMPLE About how long is this ribbon?

A paper clip is about 1 inch long, so 2 paper clips are about 2 inches. Estimate how many paper clips it will take to reach the end of the ribbon. A good estimate is 4 inches.

You can use a measuring tool like a ruler to find out just how long an item is.

EXAMPLE Use an inch ruler to measure the same ribbon.

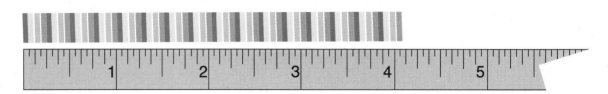

First, line up the zero mark on the ruler with the left edge of the ribbon. Then, look at the ruler's scale below the right edge of the ribbon and read the number of inches. The ribbon is a little more than 4 inches long.

Meeting the Challenge

To answer the Challenge, you have to decide about how long a pencil might be.

STEP 1: Think about whether the pencil could be 5 yards long. That length is much greater than your height! A pencil could not be 5 yards long.

STEP 2: Think about whether the pencil could be 5 feet long. That length is still greater than the height of some people. A pencil could not be 5 feet long.

The answer to the Challenge is that the pencil is about 5 inches long.

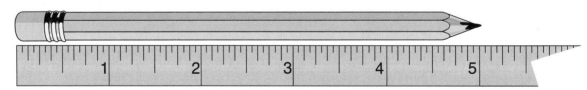

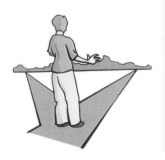

Another Way If you know the lengths of different parts of your body, you will have some handy tools for estimating lengths. For example, you might find that your hand is 4 inches across. Then you can compare your hand to something else you want to measure. Find one of your knuckles that is about 1 inch long. It can be your own inch ruler!

Name _____ Class _____ Date _____

Try It Yourself

A. Fill in the circle next to the correct answer to each multiple-choice question.

1. Which of these measurements is shorter than 1 foot (ft)?

   Ⓐ 1 yd   Ⓑ 8 in.   Ⓒ 12 in.   Ⓓ 30 in.

2. Use an inch ruler to find the length of this picture of a party horn. Which is the closest length?

   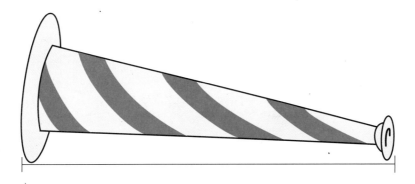

   Ⓐ 2 in.   Ⓑ 4 in.   Ⓒ 6 in.   Ⓓ 8 in.

3. Jackson cuts a 6-inch piece off an 18-inch string. How long is the piece that is left?

   Ⓐ 1 in.   Ⓑ 1 ft   Ⓒ 2 ft   Ⓓ 1 yd

4. Each child in Miss Benton's class is making a 1-yard-long paper chain. So far, Tina has made 20 inches of her chain. How many more inches does she still have to make?

   Ⓐ 4 in.

   Ⓑ 12 in.

   Ⓒ 16 in.

   Ⓓ 28 in.

Go On

5. Which of these measurements is longer than 24 inches?

    Ⓐ 1 yd   Ⓑ 1 ft   Ⓒ 2 ft   Ⓓ 2 in.

6. Use an inch ruler to find the length of this picture of a toy car. Which is the closest to the actual length shown?

    Ⓐ 1 in.

    Ⓑ 2 in.

    Ⓒ 3 in.

    Ⓓ 4 in.

7. Which of these measurements best describes the height of a cafeteria table?

    Ⓐ 2 in.   Ⓑ 30 in.   Ⓒ 10 ft   Ⓓ 3 yd

8. How many inches are in half a yard?

    Ⓐ 6 in.   Ⓑ 12 in.   Ⓒ 18 in.   Ⓓ 24 in.

B. Complete the two parts below. Show all your work.

Lisa has a bubble-gum rope that is 1 yard long. She is going to cut it in pieces to share with her friends.

Part A Lisa gives one-third of the bubble gum to her best friend, Rudy. Esteban gets half as much as Rudy. How many inches does Lisa give to Rudy and Esteban? Write your answers in the chart.

Part B Now Lisa gives 4 inches of bubble gum to Gloria and 6 inches to Dina. How many inches are left? Write your answer in the chart. Make sure that all the pieces add up to 36 inches (1 yard).

Name	Length (in.)
Rudy	
Esteban	
Gloria	4 in.
Dina	6 in.
Left over	
Total	36 in.

MEASURING LENGTH: METRIC UNITS

This lesson addresses Benchmarks MA.B.1.2.1, MA.B.1.2.2, MA.B.2.2.1, MA.B.2.2.2, MA.B.3.2.1, MA.B.4.2.1, and MA.B.4.2.2 of the Sunshine State Standards.

The Challenge

Jason's teacher gives each student one ice cream stick and a centimeter ruler.

ICE CREAM

The students must find out how much more or less than 1 decimeter long this stick is. Jason measures and says that it is 1 centimeter more than a decimeter. Is he correct?

Learning the Ropes

People throughout the world measure using **metric units.** The chart below shows some metric measures.

Metric Unit	Objects for Estimating	Number Sentences
centimeter (cm)	the width of a fingertip	10 cm = 1 dm 100 cm = 1 m
decimeter (dm)	the height of a coffee mug	1 dm = 10 cm 10 dm = 1 m
meter (m)	the distance from the floor to a doorknob	1 m = 100 cm 1 m = 10 dm
kilometer (km)	the distance a person can walk in 15 minutes	1 km = 1000 m

Math in History
The scarab beetle was a religious symbol in ancient Egypt. There is even a scarab beetle symbol in Egyptian writing. Scarab beetles are 2 to 3 centimeters in length. Scarab beetles are just one kind out of several hundred thousand species that exist today. One of the largest beetles is the South American Longhorn Beetle, which can be over 16 centimeters in length, not including its antennae!

Math in Use: Films Many science museums show films in special theaters with huge movie screens. Most of these theaters have a rectangular screen that is about 16 meters high and 22 meters wide, but this type of screen can be much larger. The biggest screens are 30 meters (almost 100 feet, or 8 stories) tall. As you watch the action on such a huge screen, sometimes it feels as if you are actually taking part in the action!

EXAMPLE What is a good estimate for the metric length of this key?

A fingertip is about 1 centimeter wide. The key is about 4 times longer than the fingertip's width. A good estimate is 4 centimeters.

EXAMPLE Exactly how long is this key? Use a centimeter ruler to measure.

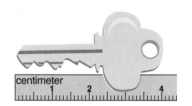

Line up the zero mark on the ruler with the left edge of the key. Read the number of centimeters. The key is 4 centimeters long.

Meeting the Challenge

To answer the Challenge, you need to measure the ice cream stick and then compare it to a decimeter.

STEP 1: Measure the length of the ice cream stick.

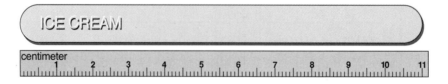

The length of the stick is 11 centimeters.

STEP 2: Compare the actual length of the ice cream stick with a decimeter.

1 dm = 10 cm

11 cm > 10 cm, so subtract to find the difference.

11 cm − 10 cm = 1 cm

The answer to the Challenge is that the ice cream stick is 1 centimeter longer than a decimeter. Jason is correct.

Try It Yourself

A. Fill in the circle next to the correct answer to each multiple-choice question.

1. Anne puts a 13-centimeter (cm) pen in her shirt pocket. Only the top part of the pen (about 3 centimeters) sticks out of the pocket. How deep is the pocket on Anne's shirt?

   Ⓐ 10 meters (m)   Ⓒ 3 decimeters (dm)

   Ⓑ 1 meter (m)   Ⓓ 1 decimeter (dm)

2. Which is the best estimate of the length of these scissors?

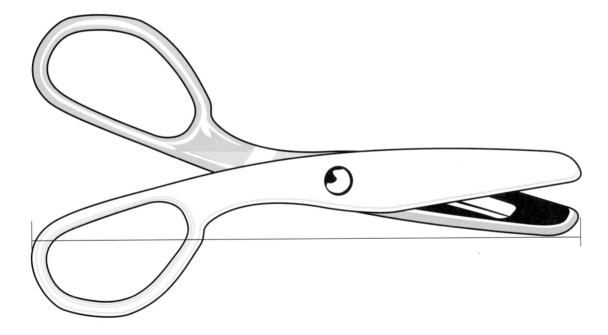

   Ⓐ 15 centimeters (cm)   Ⓒ 15 meters (m)

   Ⓑ 15 decimeters (dm)   Ⓓ 15 kilometers (km)

3. Which of these measurements best describes a tall person's height?

   Ⓐ 2 dm   Ⓑ 2 m   Ⓒ 2 cm   Ⓓ 5 m

Go On 159

4. Which of these measurements is less than 1 meter?

- (A) 100 centimeters (cm)
- (B) 75 centimeters (cm)
- (C) 10 decimeters (dm)
- (D) 15 decimeters (dm)

5. Use a centimeter ruler to measure the piece of chalk shown here. Which length below is nearest to the exact length?

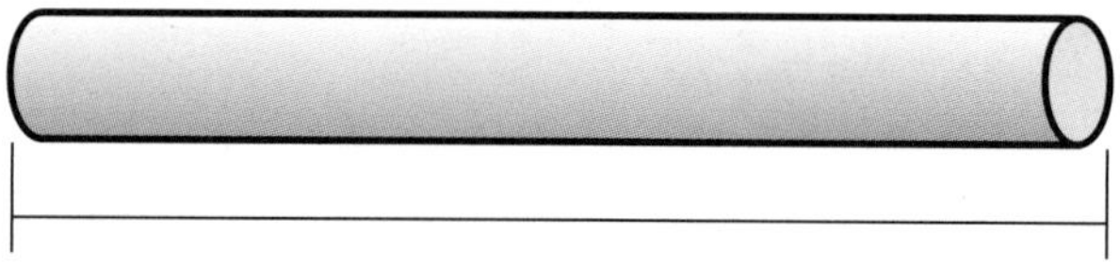

- (A) 2 cm
- (B) 4 cm
- (C) 6 cm
- (D) 8 cm

6. Which of these measurements best describes the length of a school bus?

- (A) 10 cm
- (B) 100 cm
- (C) 10 dm
- (D) 10 m

7. Which of these objects is closest to 2 meters tall?

- (A) a drinking glass
- (B) a door
- (C) a full-grown maple tree
- (D) a home computer

8. Complete the two parts below. Show all your work.

Mrs. Lawson buys a strip of cloth that is 1 meter long. She needs pieces of different lengths for a project.

Part A First, she cuts a piece that is 1 decimeter long. Then she cuts 30 small pieces, each 2 centimeters long. How many centimeters has she cut so far?

Part B How many 5-centimeter pieces can Mrs. Lawson cut from the cloth that is left?

MEASURING PERIMETER

This lesson addresses Benchmarks MA.B.1.2.1, MA.B.1.2.2, MA.B.3.2.1, and MA.C.3.2.1 of the Sunshine State Standards.

The Challenge

Becky's class is making picture frames for Grandparents Day. Becky's frame is 7 inches long and 5 inches wide. What is the perimeter of her frame?

Matt's frame is a square that is 2 decimeters long on each side. What is the perimeter of his frame?

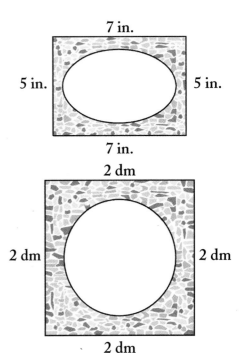

7 in.

5 in.　　　5 in.

7 in.

2 dm

2 dm　　　2 dm

2 dm

Learning the Ropes

Perimeter is the distance around the outside of a figure. To find the perimeter of a figure, add the measures of all the sides together. For a rectangle, the measure of each of the two longer sides is called the **length**. The measure of each of the two shorter sides is called the **width.**

EXAMPLE Use an inch ruler to find the perimeter of the figure to the right.

When you measure the rectangle, you should find that the length is 3 inches and that the width is 1 inch. To find the perimeter, add the measures of all the sides:

Perimeter = length + width + length + width
Perimeter = 3 in. + 1 in. + 3 in. + 1 in. = 8 in.

The perimeter of the figure is 8 inches.

Math in History

The Hermitage, a castle in Scotland, was built more than 700 years ago. At first, it was in the shape of a rectangle. Later, parts were added to the castle, and its shape was changed to look like the diagram below. How would you find the perimeter of the castle walls?

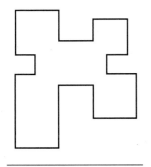

Meeting the Challenge

To answer the Challenge, you have to find the perimeter of each figure.

STEP 1: To find the perimeter of Becky's picture frame, add the lengths of all the sides.

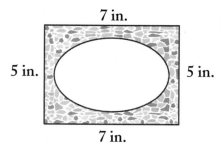

Perimeter = length + width + length + width
Perimeter = 7 in. + 5 in. + 7 in. + 5 in.
         = 24 in.

The perimeter of Becky's frame is 24 inches, or 2 feet.

STEP 2: To find the perimeter of Matt's square frame, add the lengths of the four equal sides.

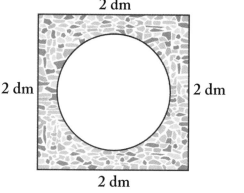

Perimeter = side + side + side + side
Perimeter = 2 dm + 2 dm + 2 dm + 2 dm
         = 8 dm

The perimeter of Matt's frame is 8 decimeters.

(In case you are wondering, the perimeter of Matt's frame is about 2 decimeters bigger than the perimeter of Becky's frame.)

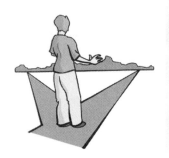

Another Way You can also use multiplication to find the perimeter. Rectangles have two lengths of the same measure and two widths of the same measure. To find the perimeter, multiply the length by 2, multiply the width by 2, and then add those two products together. A square has four sides of equal length, so multiply the length of one side by 4. Here is how to find the perimeter of Matt's square frame:

2 dm × 4 = 8 dm

Name _____ Class _____ Date _____

Try It Yourself

A. Fill in the circle next to the correct answer to each multiple-choice question.

1. What is the perimeter of this rectangle in centimeters (cm)?

   Ⓐ 7 cm
   Ⓑ 11 cm
   Ⓒ 22 cm
   Ⓓ 24 cm

   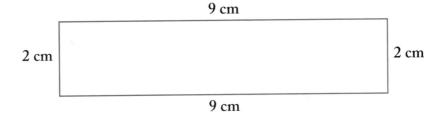

2. The measure of one side of this square is about 4 centimeters. What is the perimeter in centimeters (cm)?

   Ⓐ 4 cm
   Ⓑ 8 cm
   Ⓒ 16 cm
   Ⓓ 32 cm

3. What is the perimeter of this triangle in inches (in.)?

   Ⓐ   8 in.
   Ⓑ 24 in.
   Ⓒ 64 in.
   Ⓓ 512 in.

   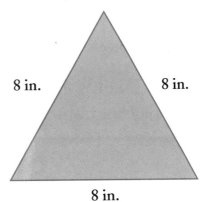

4. One side of a square window is 5 decimeters (dm) long. What is the perimeter of the window?

   Ⓐ 10 dm   Ⓑ 15 dm   Ⓒ 20 dm   Ⓓ 25 dm

Go On

5. What is the perimeter of this rectangle in feet (ft)?

Ⓐ 12 ft

Ⓑ 18 ft

Ⓒ 24 ft

Ⓓ 36 ft

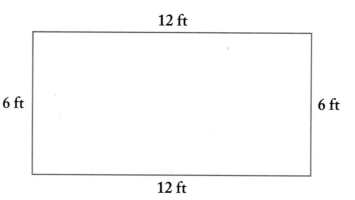

12 ft

6 ft · 6 ft

12 ft

6. The length of this rectangle is 2 inches. The width is 1 inch. What is the perimeter in inches (in.)?

Ⓐ 2 in.   Ⓒ 4 in.

Ⓑ 3 in.   ᵢ Ⓓ 6 in.

7. What is the perimeter of this shape in meters (m)?

Ⓐ 12 m

Ⓑ 9 m

Ⓒ 6 m

Ⓓ 3 m

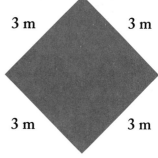

3 m   3 m

3 m   3 m

8. Complete the two parts below. Show all your work.

Tim has a piece of wood that is 40 inches long. He is going to cut it into four pieces to make a picture frame. He is trying to decide what shape to make the frame.

Part A If Tim makes a square frame, how long will each side be?

Part B If Tim makes a rectangular frame, it could be 12 inches long and 8 inches wide. On your own paper, draw another frame that he could make with 40 inches of wood. Label the lengths of the sides.

MEASURING AREA

This lesson addresses Benchmarks MA.B.1.2.1, MA.B.1.2.2, MA.B.3.2.1, and MA.C.3.2.1 of the Sunshine State Standards.

The Challenge

Dana uses square tiles to cover the top of a jewelry box. The tiles measure 1 centimeter on each side. The lid is 7 centimeters long and 6 centimeters wide. What is the area of the top of the jewelry box?

Learning the Ropes

The measurement of the space inside a flat shape is the **area.** Area is measured in square units.

This is a **square centimeter.** It is a square that measures 1 centimeter on each side.

This is a **square inch.** It is a square that measures 1 inch on each side.

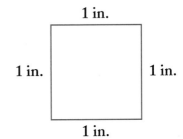

Math in History

In the past, length and area were sometimes measured in units that are hardly ever used today. You might know what a square foot is. But do you know what a square rod is? A square rod is the area enclosed by a square that is 1 rod long on each side. How long is a rod? About 1,000 years ago, the Norman invaders who conquered England decided that 1 rod would be $5\frac{1}{2}$ yards long.

Math in Use: Gold Gold is a valuable metal because it has many uses. Unlike many metals, pure gold is soft. It can easily be made into different shapes. Gold can be pounded into very thin sheets: A single ounce of gold can be hammered into a sheet that covers 250 square feet! Could 1 ounce of gold be flattened out to cover the floor of your classroom?

EXAMPLE What is the area of the grid to the right?

To find the area of a figure, divide the figure into square units and count the square units. The total area of the grid to the right is 35 square centimeters. The area of the shaded part is 15 square centimeters.

= 1 square centimeter

Meeting the Challenge

To answer the Challenge, you have to find the area of the top of the jewelry box.

STEP 1: Each tile is 1 square centimeter. To find the area covered by the tiles, count all the squares.

STEP 2: There are 42 squares. The area of the top of the jewelry box is 42 square centimeters.

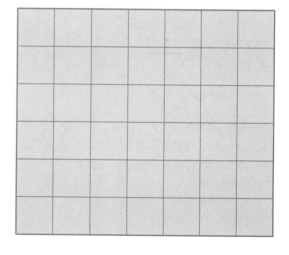

Another Way Multiplying is a quicker way to find area than counting squares. To find the area of any rectangle, multiply its length times its width. This is how to use multiplication to find the area of the jewelry box in the Challenge:

Area = length × width
Area = 7 × 6 = 42

Using multiplication instead of counting, you get the same answer: The top of the jewelry box is 42 square centimeters.

Name _____ Class _____ Date _____

Try It Yourself

A. Fill in the circle next to the correct answer to each multiple-choice question.

1. Each square in the grid to the right has an area of 1 square meter. What is the area of the shaded part?

   Ⓐ 5 square meters

   Ⓑ 6 square meters

   Ⓒ 14 square meters

   Ⓓ 20 square meters

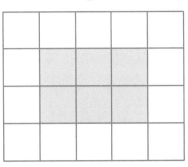

▢ = 1 square meter

2. Krissy shaded the design at right. What is the area of Krissy's design?

   Ⓐ 8 square inches

   Ⓑ 10 square inches

   Ⓒ 12 square inches

   Ⓓ 25 square inches

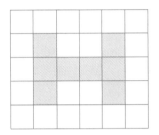

▢ = 1 square inch

3. Max is using tiles for a new bathroom floor. What is the area of the floor in square feet?

   Ⓐ 9 square feet

   Ⓑ 15 square feet

   Ⓒ 27 square feet

   Ⓓ 54 square feet

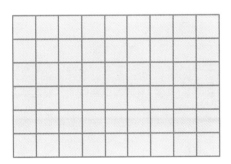

▢ = 1 square foot

Go On ▷ **167**

4. Kelly made a design using tiles. Each tile has an area of 1 square inch. What is the area of the shaded part of her design?

  (A) 12 square inches

  (B) 17 square inches

  (C) 18 square inches

  (D) 35 square inches

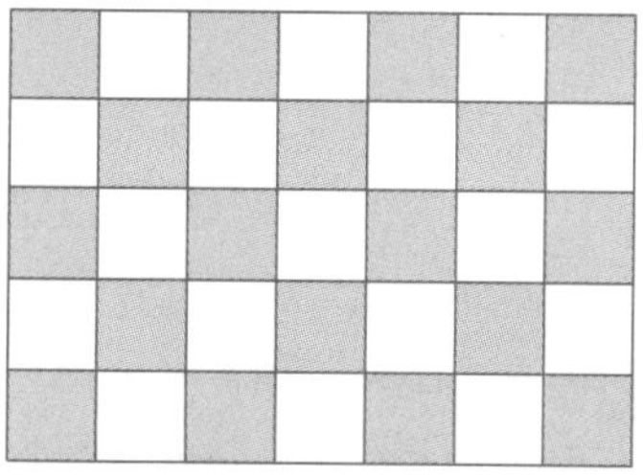

☐ = 1 square inch

5. Jasmine Taylor used tiles to spell her initials. What is the area of the tiles she used for her two initials?

  (A) 13 square centimeters

  (B) 15 square centimeters

  (C) 16 square centimeters

  (D) 63 square centimeters

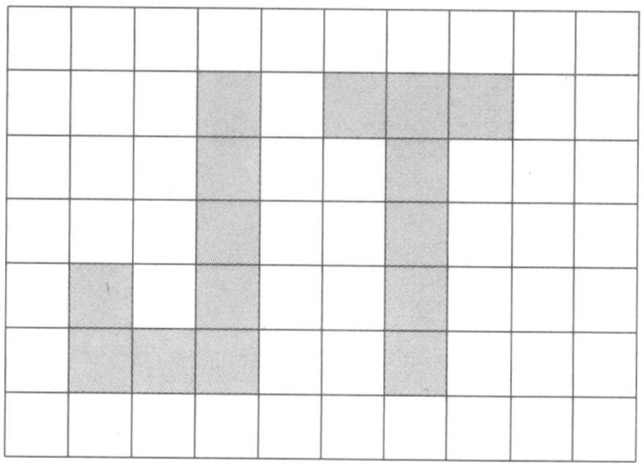

☐ = 1 square centimeter

6. Complete the activity below.

Using the grid below, draw as many different rectangles as you can that have an area of 36 square centimeters.　　☐ = 1 square centimeter

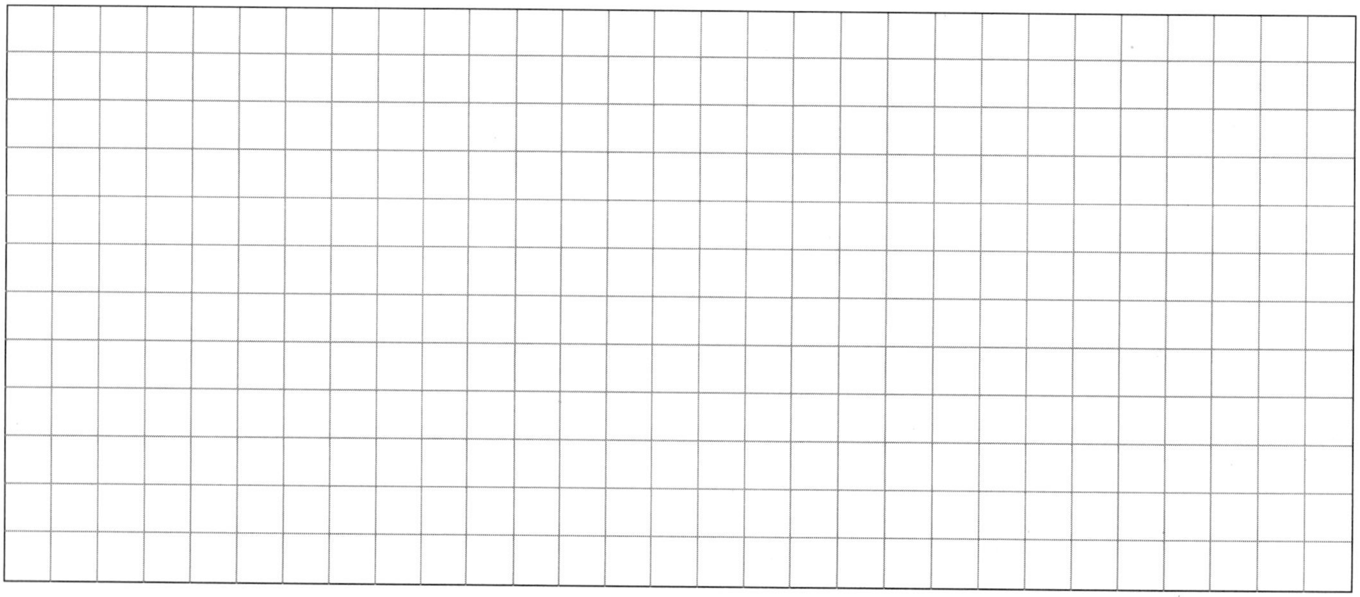

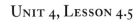

MEASURING VOLUME

This lesson addresses Benchmarks MA.B.1.2.1, MA.B.1.2.2, and MA.B.3.2.1 of the Sunshine State Standards.

The Challenge

How many blocks are in the figure to the right?

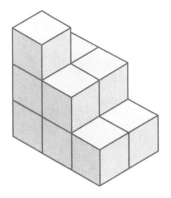

Learning the Ropes

In earlier lessons, you have learned how to measure length (one dimension) and area (two dimensions). Now you will learn how to measure **volume,** which is the amount of space taken up by an object that has three dimensions.

3 dimensions

When you measure the volume of something, you count the number of unit cubes there are in the object. Customary units of volume include the **cubic inch** (about the size of an ice cube) and the **cubic foot** (about the size of a box that can hold a basketball). Metric units of volume include the **cubic centimeter** (about the size of a number cube) and the **cubic meter** (about the volume of a refrigerator).

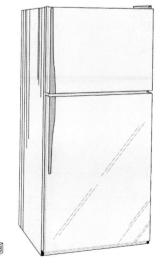

Math in History

When you look at a picture of an apple, a chair, or even yourself, what you are really looking at is a **projection**. A projection is a flat image of an object that has thickness. The image might seem to have three dimensions, but it really has only two dimensions. Each picture in this lesson is a flat image that represents an object with thickness. Girard Desargues, a mathematician from France, studied projections in the seventeenth century.

Math in Use: Pyramids What is the volume of the Great Pyramid at Giza in Egypt? It would take a long time to find out by counting blocks of stone, especially since you cannot count all the layers below the surface. There are over one million stones! To find the volume of such a large monument, you need to learn more mathematics.

Look at the pictures below. You can see one, two, or three of the sides of each cubic unit. Each figure has just one layer. The shaded sides show the way the object is facing. By counting just the shaded sides, you can count the number of blocks.

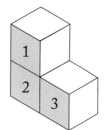 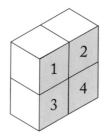 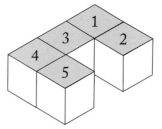

When there is more than one layer, you must count each layer by itself.

Meeting the Challenge

To find the number of blocks in the figure, you must add all the blocks in both layers.

STEP 1: Picture the figure separated into its two layers.

STEP 2: Count the blocks in each layer and add.

The answer to the Challenge is that there are 11 blocks in the figure.

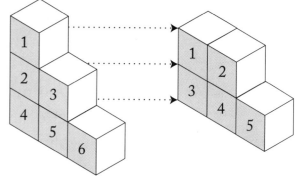

Layer 1:
6   +   Layer 2:
5   = 11

Another Way When you look at a block figure with more than one layer, it is important to remember that there may be hidden blocks. In the Challenge figure, blocks 3 and 4 in the second layer are hidden by the layer in front. You know that blocks 3 and 4 are there because blocks 1 and 2 in the second layer are sitting on top of them.

Try It Yourself

A. Fill in the circle next to the correct answer to each multiple-choice question.

1. Cho uses feet to measure length. What units would she use to measure volume?

   Ⓐ feet   Ⓑ square feet   Ⓒ square inches   Ⓓ cubic feet

2. The picture below shows two layers.

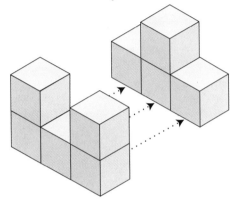

   Which of these figures shows the two layers together?

   Ⓐ

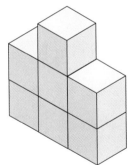

   Ⓒ

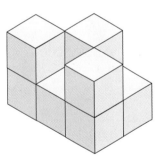

   Ⓑ

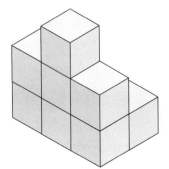

   Ⓓ

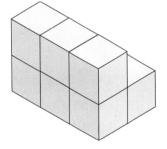

Go On   **171**

3. Which of the following stacks of blocks has the greatest volume? (Hint: To find the volume of each stack, multiply the length times the width times the height.)

Ⓐ a stack that is 2 blocks long, 2 blocks wide, and 5 blocks high

Ⓑ a stack that is 3 blocks long, 2 blocks wide, and 4 blocks high

Ⓒ a stack that is 3 blocks long, 3 blocks wide, and 3 blocks high

Ⓓ a stack that is 3 blocks long, 1 block wide, and 8 blocks high

B. Complete the four parts below. Show all your work.

Use the figure below to answer the questions. The shaded sides are the fronts of the blocks.

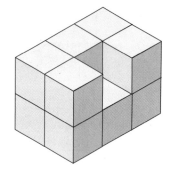

Part A How many blocks can you see the front of?

Part B How many blocks can you see the top or side of, but *not* the front?

Part C How many blocks are completely hidden?

Part D Now add up your answers from Parts A, B, and C to find out how many blocks are in the figure altogether. Another way to count them is to add the number of blocks in the top layer to the number of blocks in the bottom layer. Try it. (You can't see all the blocks on the bottom.) Are your answers the same?

MEASURING CAPACITY

This lesson addresses Benchmarks MA.B.1.2.1, MA.B.1.2.2, MA.B.2.2.1, MA.B.2.2.2, MA.B.3.2.1, and MA.B.4.2.2 of the Sunshine State Standards.

The Challenge

Pauline invites 3 friends to her house for lunch. Does she need 2 milliliters or 2 liters of juice?

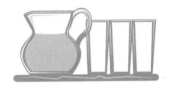

Learning the Ropes

The **capacity** of a container is the amount of liquid that a container can hold. **Liters** (L) and **milliliters** (mL) are metric units of capacity:

METRIC UNITS OF CAPACITY	
milliliter (mL)	1000 mL = 1 L
liter (L)	1 L = 1000 mL

These drawings will help you to understand the size of metric units of capacity:

A milliliter is about 10 drops of water.

A liter of water can fill about 4 medium-sized glasses.

The table to the right shows customary units for measuring capacity.

CUSTOMARY UNITS OF CAPACITY	
fluid ounce (fl oz)	
cup (c)	1 c = 8 fl oz
pint (pt)	1 pt = 2 c
quart (qt)	1 qt = 2 pt
gallon (gal)	1 gal = 4 qt

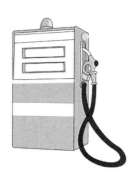

Math in Use: Converting Prices In the United States, gasoline is sold by the gallon. In many other countries, gasoline is sold by the liter. To find out how much gasoline costs in another country, you have to know how many liters there are in a gallon and how many of the other country's money units are in a dollar. For example, recently there were about 1,200 Korean *won* in a dollar. At the same time, gas cost 1,300 *won* per liter in Korea. There are 3.8 liters in a gallon. If you do the conversions, you will find that Koreans were paying over $4 for a gallon of gas!

These drawings will help you to understand the size of customary units of capacity:

1 cup   1 pint   1 quart $\frac{1}{2}$ gallon   1 gallon

Meeting the Challenge

To answer the Challenge, you need to decide how much juice four people might drink, 2 milliliters or 2 liters.

STEP 1: Consider the size of the units. Since 1 milliliter of juice is only about 10 drops of juice, two milliliters of juice is not even enough for one person.

STEP 2: Two liters of juice is enough for 8 glasses of juice. This should be enough for 4 people.

The answer to the Challenge is that Pauline needs 2 liters of juice.

Another Way You can use cubic units to help you understand capacity. A 1-centimeter cube, which has a volume of 1 cubic centimeter, can hold 1 milliliter of water. A 10-centimeter cube, which has a volume of 1000 cubic centimeters, can hold 1 liter of water.

Try It Yourself

A. Fill in the circle next to the correct answer to each multiple-choice question.

1. Which is the best estimate of the capacity of a large mug of cocoa?

   Ⓐ 2 c   Ⓑ 2 pt   Ⓒ 2 qt   Ⓓ 2 gal

2. Which is the best estimate of the capacity of a kitchen sink?

   Ⓐ 10 mL   Ⓑ 100 mL   Ⓒ 10 L   Ⓓ 1000 L

3. Which is the best estimate of the capacity of a test tube of liquid?

   Ⓐ 5 fl oz

   Ⓑ 5 c

   Ⓒ 5 qt

   Ⓓ 5 gal

4. Which unit would you use to measure the amount of juice in a large punch bowl?

   Ⓐ fluid ounces

   Ⓑ milliliters

   Ⓒ gallons

   Ⓓ cubic feet

5. Which unit of measure would you use to measure the capacity of a car's gas tank?

   Ⓐ gallons   Ⓑ feet   Ⓒ cups   Ⓓ fluid ounces

Go On

6. Which is the best estimate of the capacity of a water bucket?

ⓐ 2 qt   ⓑ 2 gal   ⓒ 50 gal   ⓓ 200 gal

7. Which is the best estimate of the capacity of a bathtub?

ⓐ 10 mL   ⓑ 100 mL   ⓒ 1 L   ⓓ 100 L

8. You travel to a country where gasoline is sold by the liter. There are about 4 liters in 1 gallon. You know that your gas tank can hold about 20 gallons of gas. About how many liters of gas would it take to fill your tank?

ⓐ 5 L   ⓑ 10 L   ⓒ 40 L   ⓓ 80 L

B. Complete the two parts below. Show all your work.

Gretchen's mother sends her to the store to buy $1\frac{1}{2}$ gallons of orange juice. The store offers the following deals on orange juice:

1 gallon $3.89 $\frac{1}{2}$ gallon $1.97   1 quart $1.09

Part A Show three different ways that Gretchen could buy jugs of orange juice to equal $1\frac{1}{2}$ gallons.

Part B Tell which combination of containers would be the cheapest. Explain your answer.

MEASURING MASS AND WEIGHT

This lesson addresses Benchmarks MA.B.1.2.1, MA.B.1.2.2, MA.B.2.2.1, MA.B.2.2.2, MA.B.3.2.1, and MA.B.4.2.2 of the Sunshine State Standards.

Math in History

Sir Isaac Newton (1642–1727), studied how gravity pulls planets toward each other. This knowledge helped astronomers to find the planet Uranus in 1781, the planet Neptune in 1846, and finally the planet Pluto in 1930.

The Challenge

Leah and Jon have designed a computer that will work on the moon. Their computer weighs 132 pounds on Earth. It has a mass of 60 kilograms. Gravity on the moon is one-sixth as strong as it is on Earth.

What will the mass of their computer be on the moon? What will its weight be?

Learning the Ropes

Mass is a measure of how much stuff an object is made of. The mass of an object is the same no matter where it is.

Gravity is the force that pulls everything toward the Earth. The amount of this pull is the **weight** of an object. The more mass an object has, the greater its weight. If you go to another planet where the gravity is stronger or weaker, you will weigh more or less, but your mass will stay the same.

Mass is measured in metric units like grams and kilograms. A paper clip has a mass of about 1 gram (g). A quart of milk has a mass of about 1 kilogram (kg).

Weight is measured in customary units like ounces (oz), pounds (lb), and tons (T). An adult eyeball and one serving of dry cereal each weigh about 1 ounce. A furry chinchilla or a soccer ball weighs about 1 pound. A sperm whale calf, an average iron safe, and a small car all weigh about 1 ton.

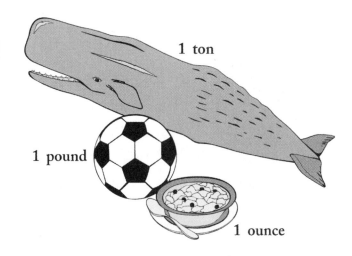

1 ton

1 pound

1 ounce

Meeting the Challenge

To answer the Challenge, you must figure out the mass and weight of the computer on the moon.

STEP 1: Figure out the mass. The mass of an object does not depend on gravity. It stays the same no matter where the object is. The mass of the computer will still be 60 kilograms.

STEP 2: Figure out the weight. On Earth, the computer weighs 132 pounds. On the moon, gravity is one-sixth as strong, so the computer will weigh one-sixth as much. You can use a calculator to divide 132 by 6. The computer will weigh 22 pounds on the moon.

Another Way Mass and weight are different measures, but you can still compare them on Earth. The force of gravity is pretty much the same everywhere on Earth. Something that has a mass of 1 kilogram will weigh about $2\frac{1}{5}$ pounds anywhere on Earth.

Name _____ Class _____ Date _____

Try It Yourself

A. Fill in the circle next to the correct answer to each multiple-choice question.

1. Which unit is *not* a measure of weight?

   Ⓐ ounce   Ⓑ pound   Ⓒ kilogram   Ⓓ ton

2. Which is the best estimate of the weight of an elephant?

   Ⓐ   3 ounces (oz)
   Ⓑ   5 pounds (lb)
   Ⓒ 50 pounds (lb)
   Ⓓ   5 tons (T)

3. Which is the best estimate of the mass of an elephant?

   Ⓐ   5 grams (g)
   Ⓑ   5 kilograms (kg)
   Ⓒ   500 grams (g)
   Ⓓ 5000 kilograms (kg)

4. An astronaut brings a rock from the moon back to Earth. The rock weighs 1 pound on the moon. How much does it weigh on Earth?

   Ⓐ $\frac{1}{6}$ lb   Ⓑ 1 lb   Ⓒ 6 lb   Ⓓ 16 lb

5. What would be the mass of a 600-kilogram statue on the moon?

   Ⓐ 600 kg   Ⓑ 100 kg   Ⓒ 60 kg   Ⓓ 10 kg

6. Which is the best estimate of the mass of a piece of paper?

   Ⓐ 2 g   Ⓑ 200 g   Ⓒ 2 kg   Ⓓ 20 kg

Go On →

7. White plastic foam is a material that floats. One cubic foot of it weighs about 1 pound. Finish this sentence:

One cubic foot of iron

- Ⓐ weighs less than 1 cubic foot of white plastic foam.
- Ⓑ weighs the same as 1 cubic foot of white plastic foam.
- Ⓒ weighs more than 1 cubic foot of white plastic foam.
- Ⓓ has the same mass as 1 cubic foot of white plastic foam.

8. Girard ate three bowls of dry cereal. About how much cereal did he eat?

Ⓐ 1 oz   Ⓑ 3 oz   Ⓒ 1 lb   Ⓓ 3 lb

9. What is the best estimate of the mass of a newborn baby?

- Ⓐ   3 g
- Ⓑ 30 g
- Ⓒ   3 kg
- Ⓓ 300 kg

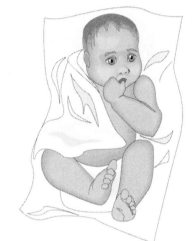

10. Complete the two parts below. Show all your work.

The scale to the right shows a book and a 2-pound bag balancing a 5-pound bag. Use the scale to answer the questions.

Part A About how many pounds does the book in the picture weigh?

Part B Suppose you had 11 pounds on one side of the scale. What combination of books and 2-pound bags would balance the 11 pounds? Explain your answer.

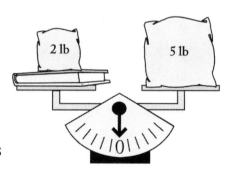

MEASURING TIME

This lesson addresses Benchmarks MA.B.1.2.1, MA.B.1.2.2, MA.B.3.2.1, and MA.B.4.2.2 of the Sunshine State Standards.

Math in History
People first measured time by watching shadows that objects made during the day. Around 3500 B.C., small towers were used to divide the time into morning and afternoon. Later, people used sundials to split the day into hours. Eventually, people made clocks that used the flow of dripping water or the pull of a heavy weight. In about 1510, clocks that used springs were developed.

The Challenge

Kendall leaves for school when the kitchen clock shows this time. He arrives at school at 7:55 A.M.

How much time passes from the time Kendall leaves home until he arrives at school?

Learning the Ropes

We use units of **time** to measure how long it takes for something to happen. Look at the chart below.

Time Units	Equal Time Periods	Time Units	Equal Time Periods
second (sec)	60 sec = 1 min	week (wk)	1 wk = 7 days 52 wk + 1 or 2 days = 1 yr
minute (min)	1 min = 60 sec 60 min = 1 hr	month (mo)	1 mo = 31 days, except for 30 days in April, June, September, November; 28 or 29 days in February
hour (hr)	1 hr = 60 min 24 hr = 1 day		
day	1 day = 24 hr 7 days = 1 wk 365 or 366 days = 1 yr	year (yr)	1 yr = 365 or 366 days 1 yr = 52 wk + 1 or 2 days 1 yr = 12 mo

Both of these clocks show the time 6:43. This time is read as "six forty-three." On the clock with hands, read the number before the smaller hand first. That tells the hour. The little lines on the clock face show the minutes.

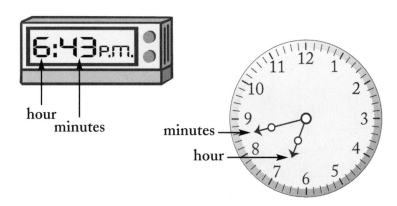

To find how many minutes pass between two times, subtract. To find what time it is after some time passes, add the time that passes to the starting time.

EXAMPLE Ana begins her piano practice at 2:05 P.M. She finishes 30 minutes later. What time does she finish her practice?

Add 30 minutes to the time she starts her practice: 2:05 + 30 = 2:35. Ana finishes her practice at 2:35 P.M.

Meeting the Challenge

To answer the Challenge, you must find how much time it takes Kendall to go from his house to school.

STEP 1: Read the time on the clock at home. Kendall leaves home at 7:35 A.M.

STEP 2: Subtract to find the time that passes while he is going to school: 7:55 − 7:35 = 20

It takes Kendall 20 minutes from the time he leaves home to arrive at school.

Another Way You can also count on from the starting time to find how much time goes by. Count on by fives and ones.

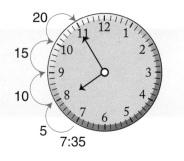

Try It Yourself

4.8 Measuring Time

A. Fill in the circle next to the correct answer to each multiple-choice question.

1. What time is shown on the clock below?
   Ⓐ 2:30
   Ⓑ 2:33
   Ⓒ 2:35
   Ⓓ 2:38

2. Which of the following best describes the time shown on the clock below?
   Ⓐ It is 11:57.
   Ⓑ It is between 11:50 and 11:55.
   Ⓒ It is between 12:55 and 1:00.
   Ⓓ It is 1:57.

3. Ray's class begins lunch at the time shown on the clock below. Lunch ends at 12:25 P.M. How long is Ray's lunch period?
   Ⓐ 5 minutes
   Ⓑ 20 minutes
   Ⓒ 25 minutes
   Ⓓ 5 hours

4. Miss Riley's class started taking a test at 9:10 A.M. They put their pencils down at 9:45 A.M. How long did they work on the test?
   Ⓐ 25 min   Ⓑ 35 min   Ⓒ 45 min   Ⓓ 55 min

5. Which of these clocks shows 2:18?

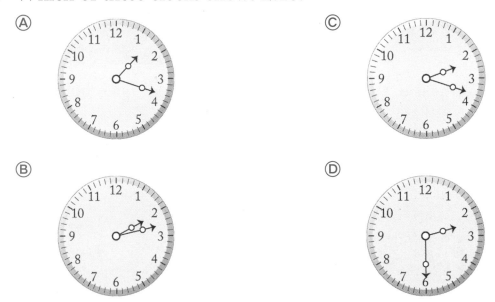

Ⓐ

Ⓒ

Ⓑ

Ⓓ

ⅠВ. Complete the four parts below. Show all your work.

Study the clocks to answer the questions in Parts A–D.

Part A Lon got home from school at 3:15. Then he played outside until the time on clock A. How long did he play?

Part B Lon worked on math from the time on clock A until the time on clock B. How long did he work on math?

Part C How much time has gone by from the time on clock B to the time shown on clock C?

Part D Lon helped his mom in the kitchen from the time on clock C until the time on clock D. How long did he help her?

Clock A   Clock B   Clock C   Clock D

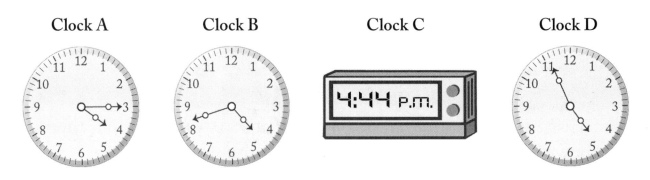

MEASURING TEMPERATURE

This lesson addresses Benchmarks MA.B.1.2.1, MA.B.1.2.2, MA.B.3.2.1, and MA.B.4.2.2 of the Sunshine State Standards.

Math in History

In 1742, Swedish astronomer Anders Celsius wrote about a temperature scale that would later have his name. He used the temperature of melting ice or snow and the temperature of boiling water as the fixed points on his scale. At first, the Celsius scale used 100° as the freezing point and 0° as the boiling point. Later, the numbers for these points were reversed.

The Challenge

The Celsius thermometer to the right is outside Tanya's window at home. Does she need to wear a heavy jacket if she goes outside to play?

Tanya is going to visit her grandparents. The Fahrenheit thermometer shows the temperature at her grandparents' house. Should Tanya pack her bathing suit or her snowshoes?

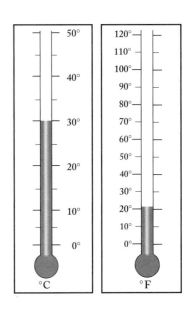

Learning the Ropes

Temperature tells how hot or cold something is. You can measure temperature in **degrees Fahrenheit (°F)** or in **degrees Celsius (°C). Thermometers** are instruments that measure temperature.

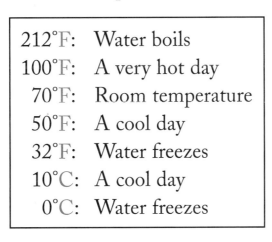

212°F:	Water boils
100°F:	A very hot day
70°F:	Room temperature
50°F:	A cool day
32°F:	Water freezes
10°C:	A cool day
0°C:	Water freezes

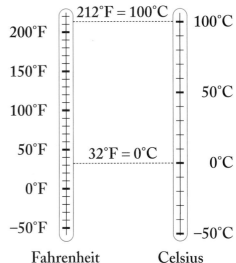

Fahrenheit   Celsius

To read a thermometer, find the number closest to the top of the liquid in the tube. Then, count up or down to the level of the liquid. Name the temperature and the scale. This thermometer shows that the temperature is 16°F, which is read "sixteen degrees Fahrenheit."

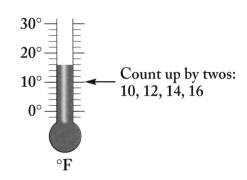

Meeting the Challenge

To answer the Challenge, read the temperature on each thermometer. Decide how hot or cold it is outside.

STEP 1: Read the temperature on the thermometer outside Tanya's window. The temperature is 30°C, which is between 22°C (room temperature) and 37°C (a very hot day). Tanya will not need a heavy jacket outside.

STEP 2: Read the temperature on the thermometer at Tanya's grandparents' house. The temperature is below 32°F. Water freezes at 32°F, so that is a cold temperature. There could be snow on the ground, so Tanya should pack her snowshoes.

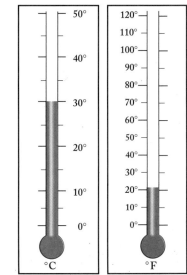

Another Way One way to understand a temperature is to compare it to these temperatures:

    room temperature (comfortably warm)

    water's freezing point (very cold)

    water's boiling point (very hot)

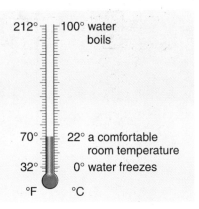

Name _____ Class _____ Date _____

Try It Yourself

A. Fill in the circle next to the correct answer to each multiple-choice question.

1. What is the temperature shown on this thermometer?
   - Ⓐ 70°F
   - Ⓑ 74°F
   - Ⓒ 78°F
   - Ⓓ 80°F

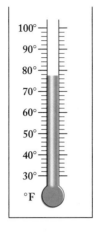

2. Which of the following best describes the temperature shown on this Celsius thermometer?
   - Ⓐ a nice summer day
   - Ⓑ a very hot summer day
   - Ⓒ a cool fall day
   - Ⓓ a very cold winter day

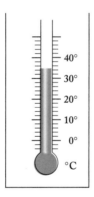

3. Agnes measures the water temperature in the pond near her home. The water temperature is shown on the thermometer to the right. How many more degrees must the water temperature drop before the water will freeze?
   - Ⓐ 16°F
   - Ⓑ 32°F
   - Ⓒ 48°F
   - Ⓓ 52°F

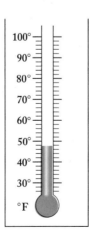

Go On ⟩ **187**

4. What is the temperature shown on this Celsius thermometer?

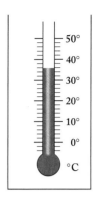

Ⓐ 28°C

Ⓑ 32°C

Ⓒ 36°C

Ⓓ 40°C

5. Which of the following best describes the temperature shown on this Fahrenheit thermometer?

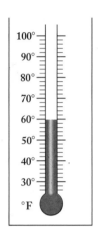

Ⓐ a cool spring day

Ⓑ a very cold winter day

Ⓒ a warm summer day

Ⓓ a very hot summer day

6. Complete the two parts below.

The scales to the right show Fahrenheit temperatures on one side and the matching Celsius temperatures on the other side.

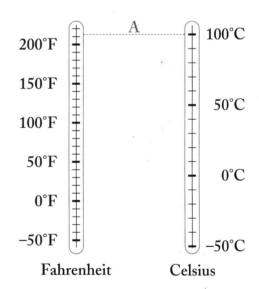

Part A For each item below, draw a line between the temperatures described. Label each connecting line with the correct letter for your answer. The first one has been done for you.

• The boiling point of water (A)

• The freezing point of water (B)

• A hot summer day (C)

• A chilly fall day (D)

Part B Which would be a greater drop in temperature, 30°F or 30°C? Explain your answer. Use your own paper.

COUNTING MONEY

This lesson addresses Benchmarks MA.A.1.2.3, MA.A.2.2.1, MA.B.1.2.2, and MA.B.3.2.1 of the Sunshine State Standards.

The Challenge

Raoul buys a notebook for $2.47. He pays for it with exact change. What are the fewest bills and coins he can use?

Suppose Raoul gives the clerk $5. How much change should the clerk give him?

Math in History
Quarters, half-dollars, dollar coins, dimes, and pennies began to be used in the 1790s. The nickel (5-cent piece) first appeared in 1866. Did you know that other coins were used at different times in U.S. history? The half-cent was made from 1793 to 1857. The 2-cent piece was used from 1864 to 1873. The 3-cent piece was used from 1851 to 1873. A 20-cent piece was used for only three years, from 1875 to 1878.

Learning the Ropes

Our system of money uses dollars and cents. One dollar is worth 100 cents. Here are some bills and their values:

first issued October, 2003
new $20 bill
twenty dollars ($20.00)

$10 bill
ten dollars ($10.00)

$5 bill
five dollars ($5.00)

$1 bill
one dollar ($1.00)

decimal point

The number before the decimal point is the number of dollars.
The number after the decimal point is the number of cents.

Math in Use: Coins The U.S. Mint makes the coins for this country. Recently, the Mint started making golden dollars and special quarters for each state. The Mint sells sets of brand-new coins, called "proof sets." For $19.95, you can buy a 10-coin set. It has 5 state quarters, a Lincoln cent, a Jefferson nickel, a Roosevelt dime, a Kennedy half-dollar, and the golden dollar. What is the face value of this proof set? Add the values:

$$\$1.25 + 0.01 + 0.05 + 0.10 + 0.50 + 1.00 = \$2.91$$

Here are some coins and their values:

dollar
one hundred cents
(100¢ or $1.00)

half-dollar
fifty cents
(50¢ or $0.50)

quarter
twenty-five cents
(25¢ or $0.25)

dime
ten cents
(10¢ or $0.10)

nickel
five cents
(5¢ or $0.05)

penny
one cent
(1¢ or $0.01)

To find the value of a group of bills and coins, start with the bills or coins that have the greatest value. Count until you have counted the bills or coins with the least value.

EXAMPLE Find the value of this set of bills and coins.

$1.00 → $1.25 → $1.50 → $1.60 → $1.65 → $1.70 → $1.75 → $1.76

The value of these bills and coins is $1.76, or "one dollar and seventy-six cents."

The amount of change you should get is the difference between the amount you pay and the cost of the item. To find the difference, subtract.

EXAMPLE Suppose you give a clerk a $1 bill for a pen that costs $0.59. How much change should you get?

Subtract the price of the pen from the amount you give to the clerk. You should get 41 cents.

$$\begin{array}{r} \$1.00 \\ -\ 0.59 \\ \hline \$0.41 \end{array}$$

New State Quarters

Quarter, front

Quarters, back

New Jersey   Massachusetts   New York   Ohio   Pennsylvania

Meeting the Challenge

To meet the Challenge, you need to count money and make change.

STEP 1: Find the fewest bills and coins that have a value of $2.47. Start with the bill of greatest value that you can use, and keep adding more money.

$1.00 → $2.00 → $2.25 → $2.35 → $2.45 → $2.46 → $2.47

STEP 2: To find the change the clerk should give Raoul, subtract the price of the notebook from $5.00.

$$\begin{array}{r} \$5.00 \\ -\ 2.47 \\ \hline \$2.53 \end{array}$$

The answer to the Challenge is that Raoul can pay $2.47 with two $1 bills, 1 quarter, 2 dimes, and 2 pennies. If he pays for the notebook with a $5 bill, he should get $2.53 in change.

Another Way Another way to find the amount of change is to start with the cost of the item and count up.

$2.47 + + +

= $2.50   = $3.00   = $5.00

Raoul should get 3 pennies, 2 quarters, and 2 dollars ($2.53).

Try It Yourself

A. Fill in the circle next to the correct answer to each multiple-choice question.

1. What is the value of this set of bills and coins?

   Ⓐ $1.43   Ⓑ $1.53   Ⓒ $1.58   Ⓓ $1.63

2. Study this set of coins.

   Which set of coins below has the same value?

   Ⓐ    Ⓒ

   Ⓑ    Ⓓ

3. If you use exact change, which set of coins and bills could you use to pay for a book that costs $4.90?
   Ⓐ 4 $1 bills, 2 quarters, 3 dimes
   Ⓑ 4 $1 bills, 2 quarters, 4 dimes
   Ⓒ 4 $1 bills, 3 quarters, 2 nickels
   Ⓓ 4 $1 bills, 3 quarters, 2 dimes

4. Which set of bills and coins makes $1.51?
   Ⓐ 1 $1 bill, 1 half dollar, 1 penny
   Ⓑ 1 $1 bill, 4 dimes, 3 nickels, 1 penny
   Ⓒ 1 $1 bill, 2 quarters, 1 dime, 1 penny
   Ⓓ 1 $1 bill, 3 quarters, 1 dime, 1 penny

Go On

5. Which set of bills and coins has the greatest value?

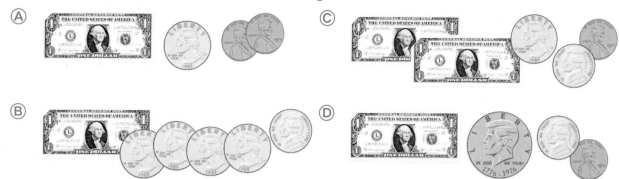

6. Which set of coins has a different value from the other sets in this group?

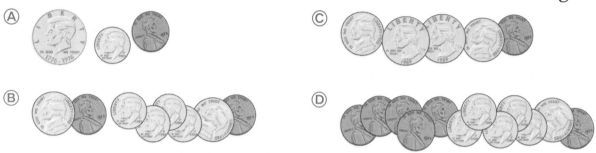

7. Chad had a $1 bill and 8 coins in his pocket. Altogether, he had $1.82. What coins could he have had in his pocket?

Ⓐ 1 half dollar, 6 nickels, 2 pennies

Ⓑ 2 quarters, 1 dime, 3 nickels, 2 pennies

Ⓒ 2 quarters, 2 dimes, 2 nickels, 2 pennies

Ⓓ 3 half dollars, 3 dimes, 2 pennies

8. Complete the three parts below. Show all your work. Use your own paper.

You and your mom go to the store to buy school supplies.

Part A You buy a pen for 79¢. What coins make exactly 79¢?

Part B You buy a bottle of glue for $3.19. You give the clerk a $5 bill. What combination of bills and coins could the clerk give you for change?

Part C How many 29-cent pencils could you buy with $1? What coins could you get for change?

Name _____ Class _____ Date _____

1. Jolene has discovered a special rectangle. The area of the rectangle in square units is the same number as the perimeter of the rectangle in units.

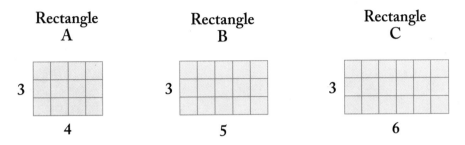

Rectangle
A

Rectangle
B

Rectangle
C

3 ⬚ 4   3 ⬚ 5   3 ⬚ 6

Which rectangle above is Jolene's special rectangle?

Show all your work. Explain how you found your answer.

✔ If you have trouble with this problem, review the following lessons:
4.3, "Measuring Perimeter"
4.4, "Measuring Area"

Unit 4

2. Kerry has made two block sculptures. Her sculptures are shown below.

 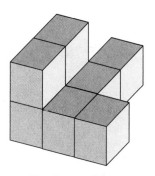

Sculpture One   Sculpture Two

For each part of this problem, show all your work. Explain how you found your answers.

Part A How many blocks are in each sculpture?

Part B If each block weighs 2 ounces, how much does each sculpture weigh?

✔ If you have trouble with this problem, review the following lessons:
4.5, "Measuring Volume"
4.7, "Measuring Mass and Weight"

ORGANIZING DATA: BAR GRAPHS

This lesson addresses Benchmark MA.E.1.2.1 of the Sunshine State Standards.

The Challenge

Mr. Gomez bought a guinea pig for his class. The students voted to name this class pet. Use the data in the chart below to create a bar graph.

Math in History

In 1811, the German explorer Alexander von Humboldt created the first known bar graph. In 1844, Charles Joseph Minard, a French mapmaker, used a bar graph to show information on transportation. Minard's graphic table showed bars divided into several colors.

Name	Number of Votes
Fluffy	8
Patch	9
Monster	11

Learning the Ropes

When you count votes for a favorite sport or find the number of minutes students spend on homework, you are collecting data. **Data** is information based on facts. There are usually numbers in data.

To make sense of the data you collect, you can organize it in a **table,** or **chart,** like the one to the right. This table shows how ten students voted for their favorite of three sports. You can see easily that most of those students like soccer best.

FAVORITE SPORTS	
Sport	**Votes**
Basketball	3
Hockey	1
Soccer	6

Math in Use: Health Care Health workers keep charts about children's health. Charts can show how many children are getting sick from certain diseases each year. If a chart shows that many children are getting measles or whooping cough, for example, then doctors will know that they need to do more to protect their patients from those diseases.

Sometimes a picture makes data easier to understand. A **graph** is a kind of picture that shows data. One type of graph is a **bar graph,** like the one to the right. Bar graphs label the categories on one side, or **axis,** and the numbers on the other axis. A bar extending from each label shows the data.

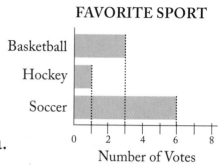

Note that the scale on the bottom of the graph is marked by twos. To show the one vote for hockey, the bar goes halfway between 0 and 2. To show the three votes for basketball, the bar goes halfway between 2 and 4.

Meeting the Challenge

To answer the Challenge, you have to use the data in the chart to set up a bar graph.

STEP 1: Write the names for the guinea pig on the side of the bar graph. Label the bottom of the graph "Number of Votes." Make a mark along the bottom for each number from 1 to 12. As on the graph above, you may label just the even numbers. Title the graph, "Class Pet Names."

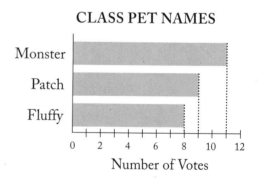

STEP 2: Draw a bar from each name to the number of votes for that name.

Another Way The graph above shows the bars going left to right. You can show the same data using bars that go up from the bottom. (Numbers are on the side now.) This kind of bar graph can be called a **column graph.**

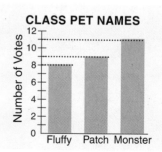

Name _____ Class _____ Date _____

Try It Yourself

A. Fill in the circle next to the correct answer to each multiple-choice question.

The graph below shows the favorite summer activities of a group of third graders. Use the graph to answer questions 1 and 2.

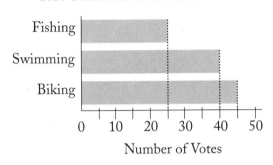

FAVORITE SUMMER ACTIVITY

1. How many students voted for biking?
   Ⓐ 25　　　Ⓑ 40　　　Ⓒ 41　　　Ⓓ 45

2. How many more students voted for swimming compared to fishing?
   Ⓐ 3 more　　　Ⓑ 10 more　　　Ⓒ 15 more　　　Ⓓ 20 more

3. The graph to the right shows the number of students who signed up for after-school activities during April and May. How many more students signed up for homework in May than in April?
   Ⓐ 5 more
   Ⓑ 10 more
   Ⓒ 15 more
   Ⓓ 25 more

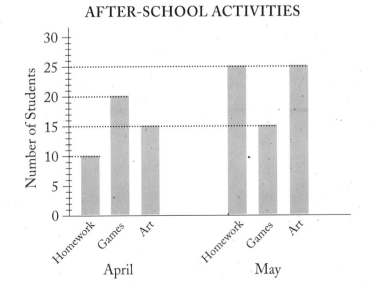

AFTER-SCHOOL ACTIVITIES

Go On ➡ **199**

The graph below shows the favorite school activities of a group of third graders. Use the graph to answer questions 4 and 5.

FAVORITE SCHOOL ACTIVITY

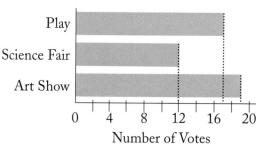

4. Which activity received the most votes?

   Ⓐ play

   Ⓑ art show

   Ⓒ science fair

   Ⓓ The play and the art show were tied.

5. How many votes did the play receive?

   Ⓐ 16   Ⓑ 17   Ⓒ 18   Ⓓ 19

B. Complete the three parts below.

The graph to the right shows the number of minutes that four students spent watching television on a Friday and Saturday. Use the graph to answer the questions in Parts A–C.

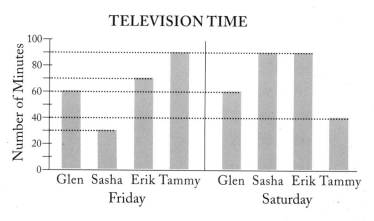

Part A Which student watched the same amount of television on Friday as on Saturday?

Part B Which student watched the most television on the two days?

Part C Which student watched less on Saturday than on Friday?

ORGANIZING DATA: PICTOGRAPHS

This lesson addresses Benchmark MA.E.1.2.1 of the Sunshine State Standards.

Math in History

From 1900 to 2000, the number of people living in Clark County, Nevada, grew from about 1,000 to over 1 million! These numbers show how the population grew from 1900 to 1940:

1900:	1,000
1910:	3,000
1920:	5,000
1930:	8,500
1940:	16,500

Suppose you wanted to display Clark County's population from 1900 to 1940 in a pictograph. What symbol would you use for the key? How many people would each symbol represent?

The Challenge

Mr. Gibson gives music lessons to small groups of students four days a week. He made a pictograph to show all the students he teaches. How many students does Mr. Gibson teach each day?

MR. GIBSON'S MUSIC STUDENTS	
Monday	🧍🧍🧍
Tuesday	🧍🧍🧍🧍🧍
Wednesday	🧍🧍
Friday	🧍🧍🧍🧍🧍🧍

Key: Each 🧍 means 4 students.

Learning the Ropes

A **pictograph** is a graph that uses pictures or **symbols** to represent data. Each pictograph includes a **key** to help you understand what each picture or symbol stands for. The pictograph below uses a symbol to show how many goals were scored by three hockey teams during the season. The key below the graph shows that each hockey puck stands for 6 goals.

To find the number of goals for each team, multiply the number of pucks by the number that each puck represents. Find the number of goals scored by the Hornets:

NUMBER OF HOCKEY GOALS	
Hornets	🏒🏒🏒🏒🏒
Falcons	🏒🏒🏒🏒🏒
Grizzlies	🏒🏒🏒🏒🏒

Key: Each 🏒 means 6 goals.

number of pictures × what 1 picture stands for = total number

$$5 \times 6 \text{ goals} = 30 \text{ goals}$$

The Hornets scored 30 goals during the season.

Math in Use: Business People who work in businesses can use pictographs to show important information. For example, the pictograph at right shows how many canoes a sports shop has sold in the first three years.

CANOES SOLD	
Year	
one	🛶 🛶
two	🛶 🛶 🛶
three	🛶 🛶 🛶 🛶 🛶 🛶

Key: Each 🛶 **means 10 canoes.**

When you see only half of a symbol, divide the number that a whole picture stands for by 2. In the pictograph on the previous page, a whole puck stands for 6 goals. The half-puck stands for 3 goals, so the Grizzlies scored 27 goals.

Meeting the Challenge

To answer the Challenge, you must understand what the symbols mean and figure out how many students Mr. Gibson teaches each day.

STEP 1: The key shows that each whole symbol stands for 4 students. To figure out what each half-symbol means, divide by 2: $4 \div 2 = 2$. Each half-symbol stands for 2 students.

MR. GIBSON'S MUSIC STUDENTS	
Monday	👤 👤 👤
Tuesday	👤 👤 👤 👤 👤
Wednesday	👤 ⵑ
Friday	👤 👤 👤 👤 👤 👤

Key: Each 👤 **means 4 students.**

STEP 2: Figure out how many students Mr. Gibson teaches each day.

number of pictures × what 1 picture stands for = total number:

Monday: $3 \times 4 = 12$ students
Tuesday: $5 \times 4 = 20$ students
Wednesday: $1 \times 4 = 4$; $4 + 2 = 6$ students
Friday: $6 \times 4 = 24$ students

Another Way When you want to compare data in a pictograph, you can line up matching symbols. The ones that are left over represent the difference between two groups. For example, in the pictograph of Mr. Gibson's music students, there are two more pictures for Tuesday than for Monday. Each picture represents 4 students, so Mr. Gibson has 8 more students on Tuesday than on Monday.

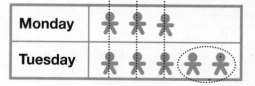

Try It Yourself

A. Fill in the circle next to the correct answer to each multiple-choice question.

The pictograph below shows Uri's stamp collection. Use the graph to answer questions 1 and 2.

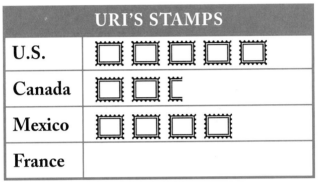

Key: Each ▢ means 8 stamps.

1. How many stamps from Mexico does Uri have?
   Ⓐ 32   Ⓑ 16   Ⓒ 12   Ⓓ 4

2. Uri buys 16 French stamps and adds this data to his pictograph. Which shows the number of symbols he uses for the 16 French stamps?

   Ⓐ ▢   Ⓒ ▢ ▢ ▢

   Ⓑ ▢ ▢   Ⓓ ▢ ▢ ▢ ▢

3. The pictograph below shows the books read by students in a book club. How many books have Marcy, Rex, and Taylor read altogether?
   Ⓐ 20
   Ⓑ 18
   Ⓒ 10
   Ⓓ 9

NUMBER OF BOOKS READ		
Marcy	📖 📖 📖	
Rex	📖 📖 📖 📖	
Taylor	📖 📖 📖	

   Key: Each 📖 means 2 books.

Go On 203

4. The pictograph below shows the total number of hits made in a season by the top three players on a baseball team. How many more hits did Ashley get than Sal?

(A) 3

(B) 12

(C) 18

(D) 21

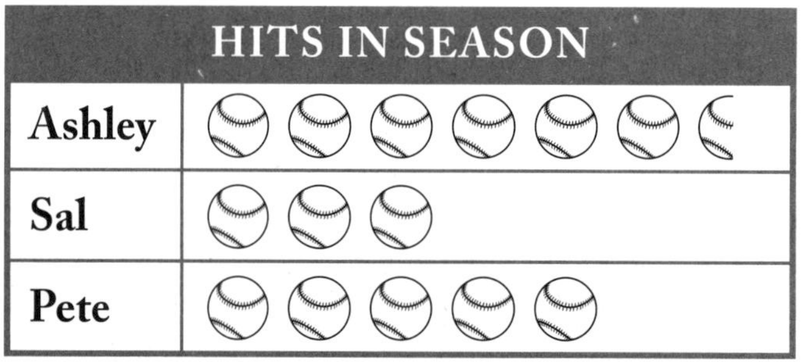

HITS IN SEASON	
Ashley	⚾⚾⚾⚾⚾⚾⚾
Sal	⚾⚾⚾
Pete	⚾⚾⚾⚾⚾

Key: Each ⚾ means 6 hits.

B. Complete the three parts below. Show all your work.

The pictograph below shows the number of items parents have agreed to bring to a school bake sale. Use the graph to answer the questions in Parts A–C.

BAKE SALE SIGN-UP	
Cakes	🎂🎂🎂🎂🎂🎂
Pies	🎂🎂
Breads	🎂🎂🎂🎂

Key: Each 🎂 means 4 items.

Part A How many pies will be brought to the bake sale?

Part B How many breads will be brought to the bake sale?

Part C Suppose that people offered to bring 42 cakes to the bake sale. How many symbols would represent 42 cakes?

ORGANIZING DATA: LINE GRAPHS

This lesson addresses Benchmark MA.E.1.2.1 of the Sunshine State Standards.

Math in History
French mathematician René Descartes (1596–1650) was the first to use a grid to display mathematical information. This great discovery helped to combine the ancient mathematics of geometry with the newer mathematics of algebra.

The Challenge

Mr. Keltzer was filling a swimming pool. Every hour, he measured the depth of the water. Look at the graph and tell how deep the water was after 3 hours.

Learning the Ropes

A **line graph** shows how data changes over time. A line graph is drawn on a grid. The markings or labels on the graph are called **scales.** The markings that go from left to right across the bottom show changes in time. The markings that go up show changes in data values.

The number line at the bottom of the grid is called the **x-axis.** The line going up the left side of the grid is the **y-axis.**

Above the grid is the title of the graph. To the left is the name of whatever units are being measured or used. On the bottom is the name of the time units that are used. To the right is a completed line graph.

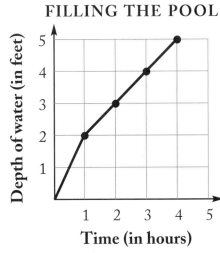

FILLING THE POOL

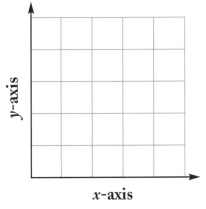

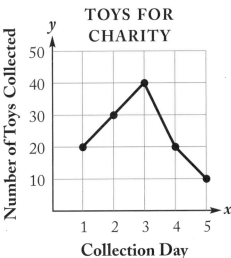

TOYS FOR CHARITY

The title tells that the line graph is about giving toys to charity. The units going up the *y*-axis show the number of toys collected each day. The units going left to right on the *x*-axis show which day the toys were collected. The dark line in the grid shows how the number of toys collected changed from one day to the next.

How many toys were collected on the third day? Find Day 3 on the *x*-axis. Now go up from Day 3 until you meet the dark line. Then go left to the *y*-axis. The point on the line that goes with 3 days also goes with 40 toys. On the third day, 40 toys were collected.

Meeting The Challenge

To answer the Challenge, you must understand the line graph.

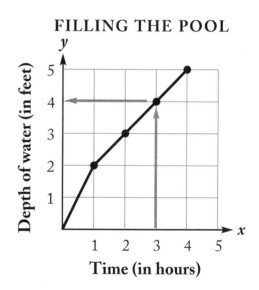

STEP 1: Find the right time. The question asks how deep the water was after 3 hours, so find 3 hours on the *x*-axis.

STEP 2: From the *x*-axis, go up until you meet the line. Then go left until you meet the *y*-axis, at 4. The depth of the water was 4 feet.

After 3 hours, the water in the pool was 4 feet deep.

Another Way Sometimes you do not need to know specific numbers; you only need to know in a general way what is happening. If you look at a line graph and see the line going upwards from left to right, you know that the amounts are increasing over time. If the line goes down from left to right, you know that the amounts are decreasing.

Name _____ Class _____ Date _____

Try It Yourself

A. Fill in the circle next to the correct answer to each multiple-choice question.

Maxine and Luke are selling toys and candy for a fundraiser. They make a line graph to keep track of how much money they raise. Use the line graph at the right to answer questions 1 to 5.

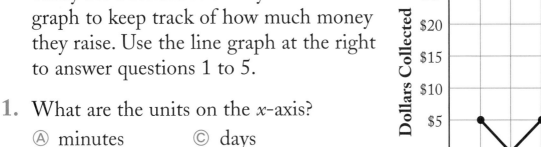

TOY AND CANDY SALE RESULTS

1. What are the units on the *x*-axis?
   Ⓐ minutes   © days
   Ⓑ hours   Ⓓ weeks

2. What are the units on the *y*-axis?
   Ⓐ number of toys   © number of dollars
   Ⓑ number of candy bars   Ⓓ number of days

3. One day it rained, and Maxine and Luke did not sell anything. What day was that?
   Ⓐ Day 2   Ⓑ Day 3   © Day 4   Ⓓ Day 5

4. How much money did Maxine and Luke make on Day 5?
   Ⓐ $5   Ⓑ $15   © $20   Ⓓ $25

5. One day was particularly nice and sunny. On that day, Maxine and Luke sold twenty dollars' worth of toys and candy. What day was that?
   Ⓐ Day 2   Ⓑ Day 3   © Day 4   Ⓓ Day 5

6. What units are shown on the *x*-axis of a line graph?
   Ⓐ units of time   © units of distance
   Ⓑ units of money   Ⓓ units of temperature

Go On

Ceta works at the aquarium. The water temperature in the large tank needs to be watched closely. Ceta measures the temperature every hour to the nearest degree and makes a line graph. Use the line graph to the right to answer questions 7 to 9.

AQUARIUM WATER TEMPERATURE

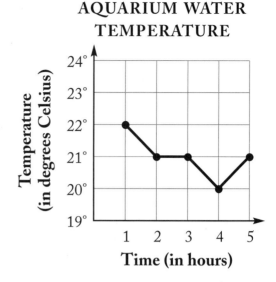

7. What is the title of the line graph?
   Ⓐ "Ceta's Measurements"
   Ⓑ "Temperature (in degrees Celsius")
   Ⓒ "Aquarium Water Temperature"
   Ⓓ "Time (in hours)"

8. What is the temperature in degrees Celsius after 5 hours?
   Ⓐ 20 degrees   Ⓑ 21 degrees   Ⓒ 22 degrees   Ⓓ 23 degrees

9. What happens to the water temperature over time?
   Ⓐ The temperature increases.
   Ⓑ The temperature decreases.
   Ⓒ The temperature stays the same.
   Ⓓ The temperature goes up and down.

🅑 Complete the two parts below.

Use the graph above to answer these questions. Explain how you got your answers.

Part A At what time was the water the coldest?

Part B At what time was the water the warmest?

RANGE, MEDIAN, AND MODE

This lesson addresses Benchmarks MA.E.1.2.2 and MA.E.1.2.3 of the Sunshine State Standards.

Math in History
The world's tallest human, Robert Wadlow, was born in 1918. He grew to be 8 feet 11 inches tall. During Wadlow's lifetime, the world's shortest human was Che Mah, who stood only 25 inches tall. This means that the range for human height is about seven feet!

The Challenge

Doctor Jacoby will do checkups on seven babies today. Here are their ages in months: 4, 5, 5, 5, 6, 8, and 9. What is the range for these numbers? What are the median and the mode for these numbers?

Learning the Ropes

People use groups of numbers every day. One kind of group comes from counting items. For example, a candy store might count the number of candy bars sold on different days. Other groups of numbers come from measuring. For example, hospitals measure the temperature of each patient.

One of the most important pieces of information about a group of numbers is the **range.** It is easy to find the range of a group of numbers. Just subtract the smallest number from the largest number.

EXAMPLE A candy store sells lollipops. Here are the numbers of lollipops they sold on Monday through Friday: 3, 4, 5, 5, and 8. What is the range?

Subtract the smallest from the largest: Range = 8 − 3 = 5.

Sometimes you want to know what number comes up most often. The number that occurs the most is called the **mode.**

EXAMPLE Here is the number of books Janelle read each week for five weeks: 1, 2, 4, 4, and 4. What is the mode?

There are three 4s and only one 1 and one 2. The mode is 4.

Math in Use: Stores People who own stores have to keep accurate counts of how many items they have sold and how many items are left. This information can tell a store owner what items are popular and what items may need to be lowered in price so that more people will buy them.

Sometimes you want to know what number comes in the middle. When a group of numbers is listed from smallest to largest, the middle number is called the **median.**

EXAMPLE Roberto has 5 flowers. He measures their height in inches and gets the numbers 6, 2, 4, 5, and 6. What is the median of the heights?

To find the median, first put the numbers in order from smallest to largest.

$$6, 2, 4, 5, 6 \Rightarrow 2, 4, 5, 6, 6.$$

Next, find the middle number. The middle number is 5. The answer is that the median height is 5 inches. This means that half of the flowers measure 5 inches or less, and half of the flowers measure 5 inches or more.

Meeting the Challenge

To answer the Challenge, you must calculate the range, median, and mode of the numbers 4, 5, 5, 5, 6, 8, and 9.

STEP 1: Find the range. The largest value is 9, and the smallest value is 4. Subtract the smallest from the largest: $9 - 4 = 5$. The range is 5.

STEP 2: Find the median. There are seven numbers. The middle number is 5.

4   5   5 ⑤ 6   8   9

STEP 3: Find the mode. The number used most often is 5.

4 ⌈5   5   5⌉ 6   8   9

The answer to the Challenge is that the range, median, and mode of this data set are all the same number, 5.

Another Way Another way to find the median is to make two lines of numbers. The first line starts with the smallest number and goes up. The second line starts with the largest and goes down. The last number is the median. Here is how the Challenge problem would look:

4   5   5   5 ← The last number left is the median.
9   8   6

Name _____ Class _____ Date _____

Try It Yourself

A. Fill in the circle next to the correct answer to each multiple-choice question.

1. After playing a game, Greg and his 4 friends each have a different number of chips. The number of chips they have are 3, 5, 6, 7, and 9. What is the **range**?

   Ⓐ 3   Ⓒ 6
   Ⓑ 5   Ⓓ 9

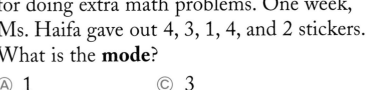

2. Students in Ms. Haifa's class get stickers for doing extra math problems. One week, Ms. Haifa gave out 4, 3, 1, 4, and 2 stickers. What is the **mode**?

   Ⓐ 1   Ⓒ 3
   Ⓑ 2   Ⓓ 4

3. Irina has 7 shells in her collection. Their lengths are 2, 3, 3, 4, 5, 5, and 5 inches. What is the **median**?

   Ⓐ 2   Ⓑ 3   Ⓒ 4   Ⓓ 5

4. Which list of numbers has a range of 5?

   Ⓐ 2, 3, 4, 5, 5   Ⓑ 3, 4, 5, 6, 7   Ⓒ 1, 2, 3, 4, 5   Ⓓ 2, 4, 4, 4, 7

5. Which list of numbers has a median of 5?

   Ⓐ 2, 3, 4, 5, 5   Ⓑ 3, 4, 5, 6, 7   Ⓒ 1, 2, 3, 4, 5   Ⓓ 2, 4, 4, 4, 7

6. Which list of numbers has a mode of 5?

   Ⓐ 2, 3, 4, 5, 5   Ⓑ 3, 4, 5, 6, 7   Ⓒ 1, 2, 3, 4, 5   Ⓓ 2, 4, 4, 4, 7

Go On →

7. Sometimes a group of numbers has more than one mode. For example, the numbers in the group 2, 2, 3, 4, and 4 have two modes: the number 2 and the number 4. Which list of numbers has two modes?

Ⓐ 2, 3, 4, 5, 5   Ⓑ 3, 4, 5, 6, 6   Ⓒ 1, 1, 3, 4, 4   Ⓓ 2, 4, 4, 4, 7

8. Here is a picture of the weights of 4 toys that Gi owns. What is the range of weights for his toys?

Ⓐ 6 ounces

Ⓑ 7 ounces

Ⓒ 8 ounces

Ⓓ 9 ounces

4 ounces   8 ounces   3 ounces   2 ounces

9. Larissa is selling caps. They come in four sizes: small, medium, large, and extra large. She keeps track of how many of each kind she sells. What number will tell Larissa which size is the most popular?

Ⓐ the range   Ⓑ the median   Ⓒ the mode   Ⓓ the total sold

B. Complete the activity below.

Carlotta has 5 dolls. She measures their heights (in inches) as 3, 5, 6, 7, and 7. What is the range, median, and mode for this set of data?

PROBABILITY

This lesson addresses Benchmark MA.E.2.2.1 of the Sunshine State Standards.

The Challenge

At a school fair, players pick a rubber duck from a swimming pool to win a prize. Each duck has a dot on the bottom. The color of the dot tells the player which prize he or she wins.

Prize	Color of Dot	Number of Ducks
stickers	red	4
popcorn	blue	10
crayons	green	4
shirt	yellow	2

If you play this game, which prize are you most likely to win? Which prize are you least likely to win? Which two prizes are you equally likely to win?

Math in History
The history of playing card games goes back hundreds of years. One of the first books of rules for card games came out in 1662. French mathematicians of the 1600s were interested in winning at card games. Their research led to the modern study of probability.

Learning the Ropes

Probability is the chance that one thing will happen instead of another. Something that has a higher probability of happening is **more likely** to happen. Something with a smaller chance of happening is **less likely.** Two things with the same chance of happening are **equally likely.**

Look at the spinners below and on the next page. Think about the probability of spinning red or yellow.

The spinner to the right has only one color—red. It is **certain** that if you spin this spinner, you will land on red. Since there is no yellow on this spinner, it is **impossible** to land on yellow.

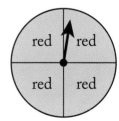

This spinner has two colors—red and yellow. Each color takes up the same amount of space on the spinner. Since the parts are equal, it is equally likely that you will spin red or yellow.

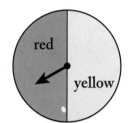

In this spinner, the red and yellow parts are not the same size. The red part is bigger than the yellow part. You are more likely to land on red than on yellow. You are less likely to land on yellow than on red.

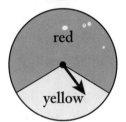

Meeting the Challenge

To answer the Challenge, you must decide which prizes are most likely, least likely, and equally likely.

STEP 1: What can happen when a player picks a duck? The dot on the bottom will be one of four possible colors: red, blue, green, or yellow.

STEP 2: Compare the number of ducks that have each color. The greatest number is 10,

Prize	Color Dot	Number of Ducks
sticker	red	4
popcorn	blue	10
crayon	green	4
shirt	yellow	2

for ducks with a blue dot. Winning popcorn is most likely. The smallest number is 2, for ducks with a yellow dot. Winning a shirt is least likely. It is equally likely that you would pick a duck with a red or green dot and win stickers or crayons.

Another Way To help you see probabilities, you can use a diagram. In the Challenge problem, there are 20 ducks in all. You could represent them as a rectangle with 20 little squares. You can see that getting a duck with a blue dot is more likely than getting any other colors.

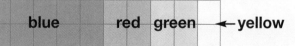

blue   red green ←yellow

Name _____ Class _____ Date _____

Try It Yourself

A. Fill in the circle next to the correct answer to each multiple-choice question.

1. The table below shows how many marbles of each color Ms. Lynch has in a bag. If you reach into the bag and pick a marble without looking, which color marble are you most likely to get?

   Ⓐ white

   Ⓑ orange

   Ⓒ black

   Ⓓ silver

Marble Color	Number of Marbles
white	19
orange	8
black	15
silver	25

2. Look at the spinner to the right and then read the answers below. Which statement is true about spinning this spinner?

   Ⓐ Red is most likely to happen.

   Ⓑ Red and blue are equally likely to happen.

   Ⓒ Red and yellow are equally likely to happen.

   Ⓓ Blue is least likely to happen.

   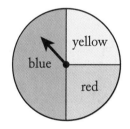

3. Look at the spinner. Which answer best describes the chance of landing on green?

   Ⓐ certain

   Ⓑ impossible

   Ⓒ most likely

   Ⓓ equally likely

   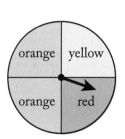

Go On ▷

4. Look at the spinner and then read the answers below. Which statement is true about spinning this spinner?

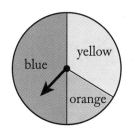

Ⓐ Orange is least likely to happen.

Ⓑ Orange and yellow are equally likely to happen.

Ⓒ Blue is certain to happen.

Ⓓ Yellow is most likely to happen.

5. Miss Crawford puts 5 green marbles in a bag. You pick one without looking. Which of the following best describes the likelihood that you will pick a green marble?

Ⓐ certain   Ⓑ impossible   Ⓒ most likely   Ⓓ least likely

6. Complete the two parts below.

At a fair, you reach into a bucket of golf balls without looking. The color of the golf ball you pick determines your prize. The chart to the right shows how many balls there are of each color.

Ball Color	Number of Balls
pink	12
red	45
orange	6
white	40

Part A Would you say it is certain, likely, unlikely, or impossible that you would pick a red ball? Explain your answer.

Part B The most expensive prizes are the hardest to get. What color ball would give you the most expensive prize? Explain your answer.

DISCRETE MATH

This lesson addresses Benchmark MA.E.2.2.1 of the Sunshine State Standards.

The Challenge

Jurawa wants to sort his marbles. He has 5 big marbles: 1 white, 1 black, 1 gray, and 2 blue ones. Jurawa also has 4 small marbles: 1 white, 1 gray, and 2 blue ones. Jurawa wants to sort his marbles into big or small ones and also into ones that are blue or not blue. How can he do this?

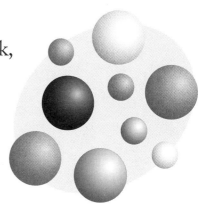

Learning the Ropes

Discrete math is mathematics about things that can be counted. Sometimes it is easier to count if you make an **organized list,** that is, you write things down in some order. For example, suppose you want to count the number of students in your school. To do this, you can make a list of names. If you write down the names in alphabetical order, you can be sure that no person is counted twice.

Alphabetical order is a way of comparing words letter by letter to see which ones come first in the alphabet. For example: *bat* comes before *cat* because *b* comes before *c* in the alphabet. When the first letters are the same, go to the second letter. The word *bag* comes before *beg* because the letter *a* comes before the letter *e*.

Adam
Amanda
Barbara
Betsy
Cheryl
Chris

Math in History
John Venn, a mathematician from England, wanted to find a better way to show how to place things in groups. By the year 1889, Venn had a method for using overlapping circles to show grouping. One of the best uses of Venn diagrams is to show how two or more groups of items relate to each other.

A **tree diagram** is used to count the number of different ways you can choose things. Suppose you are buying an ice cream cone and you want three scoops of ice cream: chocolate, vanilla, and blueberry. How many different ways can the scoops be stacked? This tree diagram shows the different ways.

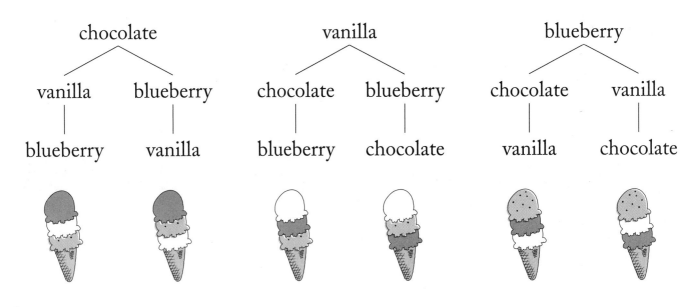

At the top of the tree diagram, you have three choices. After each of these choices, you have two choices left. They are shown in the middle of the tree diagram. After each of these choices, you have only one choice left, as shown on the last line of the tree diagram. Counting the number of branches at the bottom of the tree, you can see that there are six different ways to stack the ice cream flavors.

Math in Use: Algorithms An **algorithm** is a particular way of doing an activity. Algorithms are everywhere. A recipe is an algorithm that shows you how to cook something. A treasure map is an algorithm for finding buried treasure. The fire drill rules make up an algorithm for getting people out of a building safely. You use an algorithm every time you add, subtract, multiply, or divide!

A **Venn diagram** uses circles to sort what you are counting into like groups, or **sets.** Each circle is a group. In the Venn diagram below are animal names. The circle on the left includes animal names that have an *o* in them. The circle on the right includes animal names that have a *g* in them.

As you can see, some names like *dog, goose,* and *goat* have both an *o* and a *g* in them. Those names are in the place where both circles overlap. The word *cat* has neither letter, so it is outside of both circles.

NAMES WITH   NAMES WITH
AN *O*   A *G*

owl

dog

goose   pig   cat

moose   goat

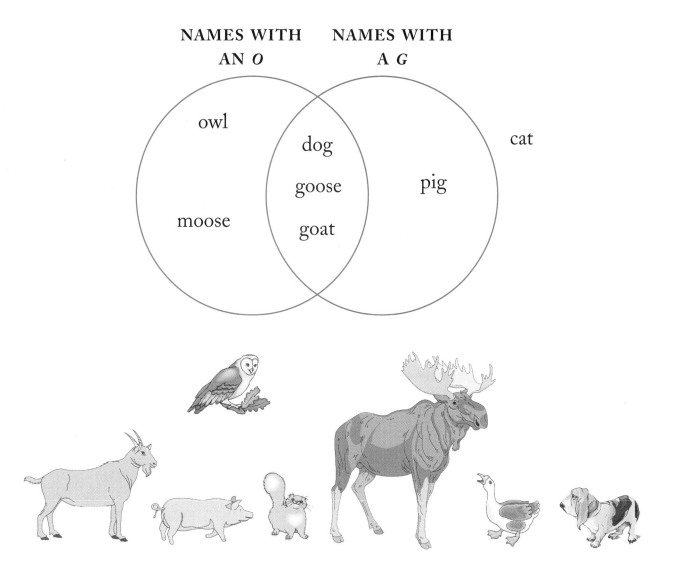

Meeting the Challenge

To answer the Challenge, you must organize the marbles using a Venn diagram.

Step 1: Draw two circles that overlap. Label one "BIG" and the other "BLUE."

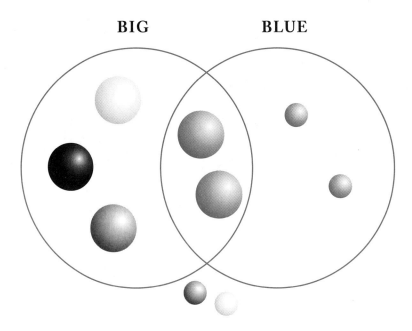

Step 2: Draw pictures of the marbles in the circles where they belong. The big black, white, and gray marbles go in the BIG circle but not in the BLUE circle. The two small blue marbles go in the BLUE circle but not in the BIG circle. The two big blue marbles go in the area where the two circles overlap. The small gray and white marbles go outside of both circles.

Another Way When you use Venn diagrams, it is important to understand what is being talked about. In the Challenge, the Venn diagram is talking about marbles. It would not make sense to ask where the number 5 fits in that Venn diagram, because you aren't talking about numbers!

Try It Yourself

5.6 Discrete Math

A. Fill in the circle next to the correct answer to each multiple-choice question.

Use the Venn diagram below to answer questions 1–3.

CHUNG'S TOYS

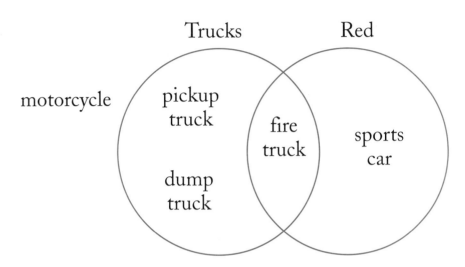

1. How many of Chung's toys are red trucks?
   Ⓐ 4   Ⓑ 3   Ⓒ 2   Ⓓ 1

2. How many of Chung's toys are trucks?
   Ⓐ 4   Ⓑ 3   Ⓒ 2   Ⓓ 1

3. Chung's uncle gives him a blue racing car. Where should it go in the diagram?
   Ⓐ with the sports car
   Ⓑ with the fire truck
   Ⓒ with the pickup truck
   Ⓓ with the motorcycle

4. Which of these lists is in alphabetical order?

Ⓐ bat, cat, rat, dog

Ⓒ bat, cat, dog, rat

Ⓑ bat, rat, cat, dog

Ⓓ bat, dog, cat, rat

5. Here is a small algorithm for flipping a coin:

Flip the coin. If it is heads, write the letter H and stop.

If it is tails, write the letter T and flip it one more time.

Then write the letter for what comes up on the second flip.

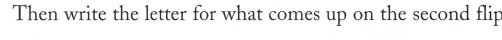

Which of these lists shows all the possible results?

Ⓐ H, T   Ⓑ H, TH, TT   Ⓒ H, T, TT   Ⓓ H, T, TH, TT

B. Complete the two parts below. Use your own paper.

Cesar has a spinner with the numbers 1 to 4 on it, as shown at the right.

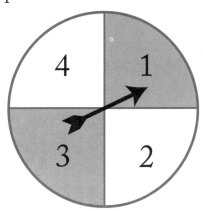

Part A Make a tree diagram of all the possible results he could get from spinning the spinner two times. How many ways can it be spun twice?

Part B Cesar is using this algorithm.

Spin the spinner. If the number is 1 or 2, write the number and stop.

If it is 3 or 4, write the number and spin one more time.

Then write the number of the second spin.

Make a tree diagram for all the possible results of Cesar's algorithm. How many results are there?

1. Jared has a bag of marbles. They come in 4 colors. The bar graph below shows how many marbles there are of each color except one. The bar for the color red has not been filled in yet.

Unit 5

JARED'S MARBLES

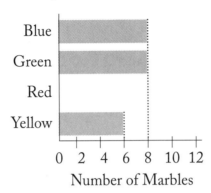

Number of Marbles

Part A Jared has 32 marbles in all. Draw a bar to show how many red marbles he has.

Part B If Jared were to pull a marble out of the bag without looking, which color would he be most likely to get? What color would be least likely? Which colors would be equally likely?

✔ If you have trouble with this problem, review the following lessons:
    5.1, "Organizing Data: Bar Graphs"
    5.5, "Probability"

Unit 5

2. The students in Mrs. Bennett's class have a flower garden. The garden is divided into four sections. The students have made a pictograph of the number of flowers in each section.

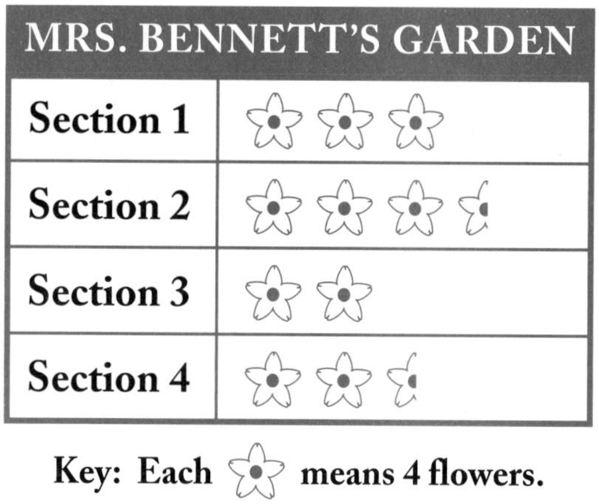

MRS. BENNETT'S GARDEN	
Section 1	✿ ✿ ✿
Section 2	✿ ✿ ✿ ✤
Section 3	✿ ✿
Section 4	✿ ✿ ✤

Key: Each ✿ means 4 flowers.

Part A Using the pictograph, find out how many flowers are in each section of Mrs. Bennett's garden.

Section 1	
Section 2	
Section 3	
Section 4	

Part B Using the flower symbols in the graph, figure out how many flowers are in all four sections of the garden. Then add up your answers for Part A. Do you get the same number?

✔ If you have trouble with this problem, review Lesson 5.2, "Organizing Data: Pictographs."

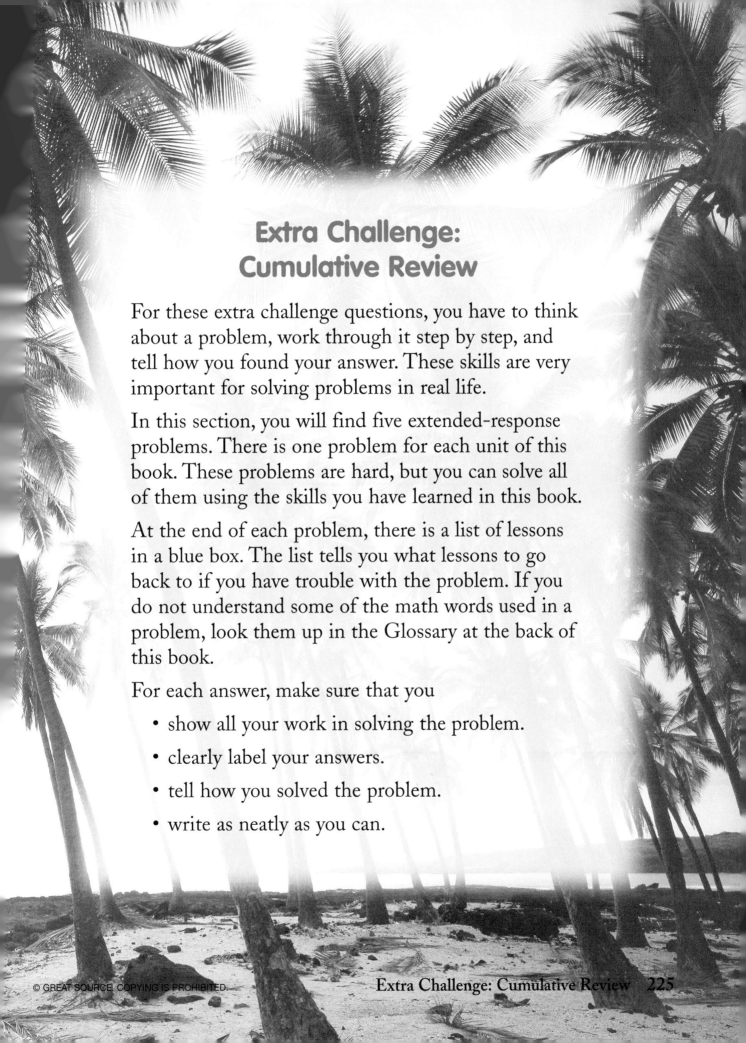

Extra Challenge: Cumulative Review

For these extra challenge questions, you have to think about a problem, work through it step by step, and tell how you found your answer. These skills are very important for solving problems in real life.

In this section, you will find five extended-response problems. There is one problem for each unit of this book. These problems are hard, but you can solve all of them using the skills you have learned in this book.

At the end of each problem, there is a list of lessons in a blue box. The list tells you what lessons to go back to if you have trouble with the problem. If you do not understand some of the math words used in a problem, look them up in the Glossary at the back of this book.

For each answer, make sure that you

- show all your work in solving the problem.

- clearly label your answers.

- tell how you solved the problem.

- write as neatly as you can.

Name _____ Class _____ Date _____

Unit 1

1. Zoe has a secret number. She has made a list of facts about the number.

> The number has 4 digits.
>
> The digit in the thousands place is a 6.
>
> The digit in the ones place is one-half of the digit in the thousands place.
>
> The digit in the tens place is one-third of the digit in the ones place.
>
> The digit in the hundreds place is two-thirds of the digit in the ones place.

Part A What is Zoe's secret number? Write the digits on the lines below.

____ ____ ____ ____

Part B Multiply 2,071 by 3. Did you get the secret number? If not, go back and check your work.

Part C Add up the digits of the secret number. What is the sum? Can the sum be divided evenly by 3? If so, what is the answer?

✔ If you have trouble with this problem, review the following lessons:
   1.1, "Place Value"
   1.6, "The Meaning of Multiplication"
   1.7, "Multiplying Whole Numbers"
   1.8, "The Meaning of Division"
   1.11, "Fractions"

2. Professor Patrick Turn has a number machine. He puts a number into the machine. The machine does something to the number and gives back a different number.

| Unit 2 |

The first chart below shows some numbers that go into and come out of the machine. The rule is "multiply by 2." When you put in a number, the machine will multiply it by 2 and give back the new number.

In	1	2	3	4	5
Out	2	4	6	8	10

Rule: Multiply by 2.

$\times 2$

Part A Look at the chart below. Try to figure out the rule.

In	1	2	3	4	5
Out	3	6	9	12	15

Rule: _____

_____

Part B Now try this one. (Hint: Multiply *and* subtract.)

In	1	2	3	4	5
Out	2	5	8	11	14

Rule: Multiply by ____ and subtract ____.

Part C Now look at the **Out** numbers in the last chart. Fill in the next three numbers in this pattern:

2, 5, 8, 11, 14, _____, _____, _____

Part D Fill in the box with the correct number:

$(6 \times 3) - \boxed{} = 17$

 If you have trouble with this problem, review the following lessons:
  2.1, "Identifying Patterns"
  2.2, "Patterns with Paired Numbers"
  2.4, "Solving Number Sentences"

3. Vanna has some squares that are all congruent. First, she makes the shape below out of 6 squares.

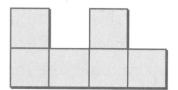

Suppose that Vanna could add 3 more squares to her shape. Show where she could put the 3 squares to make a shape that would have symmetry. Explain what it means for a shape to have symmetry.

✔ If you have trouble with this problem, review the following lessons:
   3.1, "Basic Geometric Figures"
   3.2, "Two-Dimensional Shapes"
   3.4, "Congruent Shapes"
   3.5, "Symmetry"

EXTRA CHALLENGE

4. Maxine is going to make a big batch of apple crisp. First, she needs to buy some apples, butter, and oats. She goes to the store with one $5 bill, three $1 bills, five quarters, and two dimes.

Unit 4

Part A Maxine buys a 4-pound bag of apples for $3.75, a pound of butter for $1.50, and a box of oats for $3.10. How much does she spend altogether?

Part B Does she have enough money left for a pack of gum for 85¢? Explain your answer.

Part C Maxine's recipe calls for 2 pounds of apples, $\frac{1}{2}$ cup of butter, and 1 teaspoon of cinnamon. If she uses all 4 pounds of apples, how much butter and cinnamon does she need?

Part D One-half cup of butter weighs $\frac{1}{4}$ pound. How many cups of butter are in a whole pound?

 If you have trouble with this problem, review the following lessons:
4.6, "Measuring Capacity"
4.7, "Measuring Mass and Weight"
4.10, "Counting Money"

Unit 5

5. Tara is playing a game with Alex. They have a spinner with animal names. Here is a picture of the spinner.

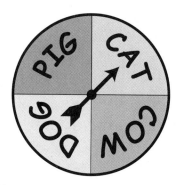

Tara goes first. She spins the spinner once and takes the first letter of the animal name she gets. Then she spins a second time and takes the second letter of the animal name she gets. Then she spins a third time and takes the third letter of the animal name she gets. She then uses the three letters in that order to make a word. What is the word she is most likely to end up with? Explain how you found your answer.

✔ If you have trouble with this problem, review Lesson 5.5, "Probability."

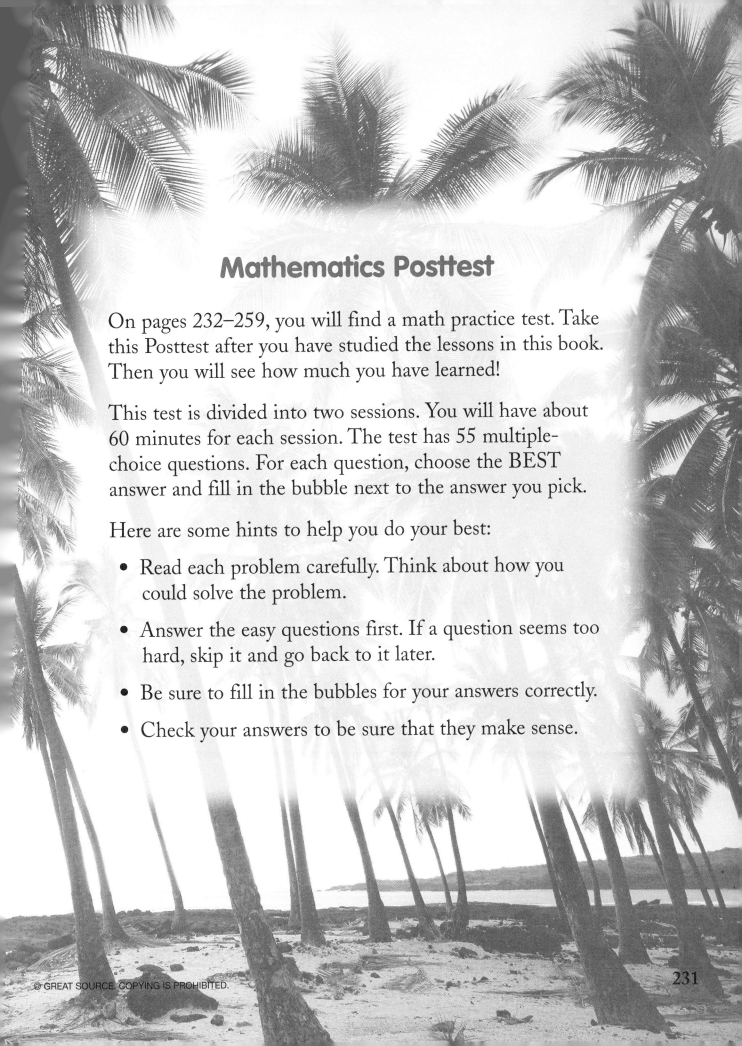

Mathematics Posttest

On pages 232–259, you will find a math practice test. Take this Posttest after you have studied the lessons in this book. Then you will see how much you have learned!

This test is divided into two sessions. You will have about 60 minutes for each session. The test has 55 multiple-choice questions. For each question, choose the BEST answer and fill in the bubble next to the answer you pick.

Here are some hints to help you do your best:

- Read each problem carefully. Think about how you could solve the problem.

- Answer the easy questions first. If a question seems too hard, skip it and go back to it later.

- Be sure to fill in the bubbles for your answers correctly.

- Check your answers to be sure that they make sense.

MATHEMATICS POSTTEST

Directions: *There are 30 multiple-choice questions in this session. For each question, choose the best answer and mark your choice in the book.*

1. In which group are **all** the letters symmetrical?

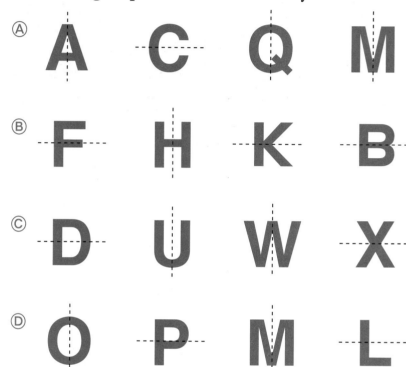

Ⓐ A C Q M

Ⓑ F H K B

Ⓒ D U W X

Ⓓ O P M L

2. What is the **best estimate** for the weight of a math book?

Ⓐ 1 ounce

Ⓑ 3 ounces

Ⓒ 5 pounds

Ⓓ 2 tons

3. Allison and Jason planted two sunflower plants. Allison's plant is 31 inches tall. Jason's plant is **twice as tall** as Allison's plant. How tall is Jason's sunflower plant?

Ⓐ 52 in.

Ⓑ 62 in.

Ⓒ 63 in.

Ⓓ 65 in.

4. How many cubes are in this figure?

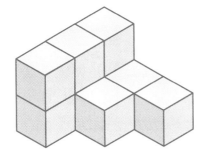

Ⓐ 7

Ⓑ 8

Ⓒ 9

Ⓓ 10

5. Samuel and Sari are working together to create a pattern using squares. How many squares will be in the next group in their pattern?

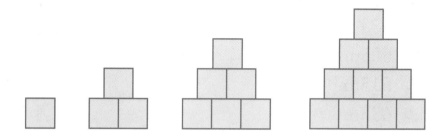

Ⓐ 5 squares

Ⓑ 14 squares

Ⓒ 15 squares

Ⓓ 21 squares

6. Holly will be leaving on vacation in 49 days. How many **weeks** is that?

Ⓐ 4 weeks

Ⓑ 5 weeks

Ⓒ 6 weeks

Ⓓ 7 weeks

7. David and his family are driving to his grandmother's house, which is 320 miles away. They drive 115 miles and take a break. How many more miles do they have to go?

Ⓐ 105 miles

Ⓑ 205 miles

Ⓒ 215 miles

Ⓓ 235 miles

8. Workers are putting tiles on the floor by the front door of the Martins' house. Each tile is 1 square foot.

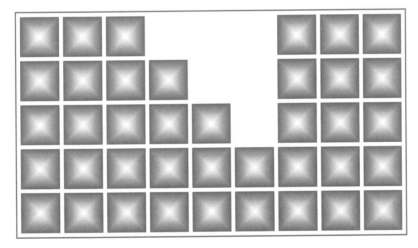

How many more square feet of tile do they need?

Ⓐ 4 square feet

Ⓑ 5 square feet

Ⓒ 6 square feet

Ⓓ 7 square feet

Go On

9. Kim has a drawer full of shirts. There are 4 blue shirts, 2 green shirts, 6 white shirts, and 1 black shirt. If he picks a shirt without looking, what are the chances that he will pick a **red** shirt?

Ⓐ certain

Ⓑ most likely

Ⓒ least likely

Ⓓ impossible

10. Use these clues to find the secret shape.

- I am a three-dimensional figure.
- I can roll.
- I have one round face and one vertex.

What am I?

Ⓐ cylinder

Ⓑ sphere

Ⓒ pyramid

Ⓓ cone

Name _____ Class _____ Date _____

11. Mrs. Brown received a basket of fruit as a gift. In the basket are apples and oranges, as shown below. What fraction of the fruits in the basket are apples?

Ⓐ $\frac{4}{7}$

Ⓑ $\frac{5}{8}$

Ⓒ $\frac{4}{3}$

Ⓓ $\frac{7}{4}$

12. Look at these figures. What must you do to the figure on the left to get the figure on the right?

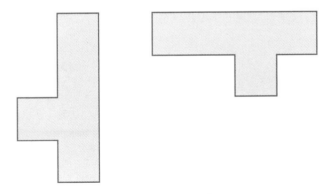

Ⓐ flip

Ⓑ slide

Ⓒ turn and slide

Ⓓ flip and slide

13. Look at the graph below. Which number pair represents the location of the library?

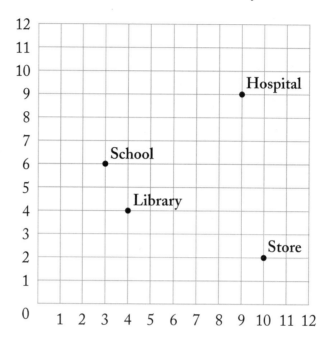

Ⓐ (4, 4)

Ⓑ (3, 6)

Ⓒ (9, 9)

Ⓓ (10, 2)

14. Which of these measurements is the **best estimate** for the length of your little finger?

Ⓐ about 5 centimeters

Ⓑ about 2 meters

Ⓒ about 5 meters

Ⓓ about 3 kilometers

15. The picture graph shows the amount of money the classes in Midwood Elementary School raised for new toys for Children's Hospital.

MONEY FOR CHILDREN'S HOSPITAL	
Grade 1	💵 💵 💵
Grade 2	💵 💵
Grade 3	
Grade 4	💵 💵 💵
Grade 5	💵 💵 💵 💵 💵 💵

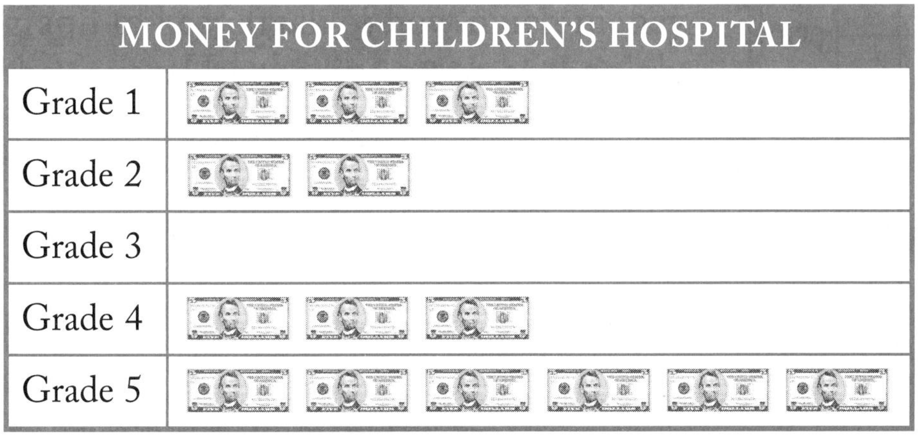

Each  💵 = $5

Grade 3 raised $25 for the hospital. What should the picture graph show for Grade 3?

(A) 💵 💵

(B) 💵 💵 💵 💵 💵

(C) 💵 💵 💵 💵

(D) 💵 💵 💵 💵 💵 💵

16. Mrs. Casey is in charge of the school buses for the town of Tyler. She needs to know how many students ride the buses every day. The chart shows the number of students from each school who ride a bus to school.

STUDENTS USING SCHOOL BUSES	
Schools	**Number of Students**
Jefferson	425
Lincoln	309
Madison	279

What is the **total number** of students who ride school buses?

Ⓐ 9,923 students

Ⓑ 1,112 students

Ⓒ 1,013 students

Ⓓ 1,003 students

17. Mrs. Randolph uses a column graph to keep track of how many cans the school recycles each month. The school recycled 8 barrels of cans in January, 4 barrels in February, 6 barrels in March, and 3 barrels in April. Which graph shows this information?

Ⓐ   **CAN RECYCLING**

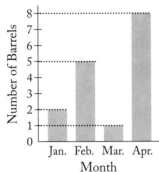

Ⓒ   **CAN RECYCLING**

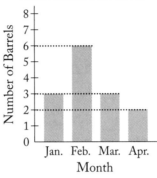

Ⓑ   **CAN RECYCLING**

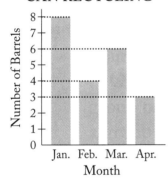

Ⓓ   **CAN RECYCLING**

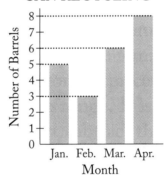

18. Sarah runs every day to prepare for a marathon. She runs the same number of miles each week. How many miles does she run in 4 weeks?

	1 Week	2 Weeks	3 Weeks	4 Weeks
Total Miles	35	70	105	?

Ⓐ 110 miles

Ⓑ 140 miles

Ⓒ 175 miles

Ⓓ 210 miles

19. Tom, Alex, Sue, and Greg live in the same neighborhood. The grid below shows where they live. Whose house is located at the point (7, 5)?

Ⓐ Tom's house

Ⓑ Alex's house

Ⓒ Sue's house

Ⓓ Greg's house

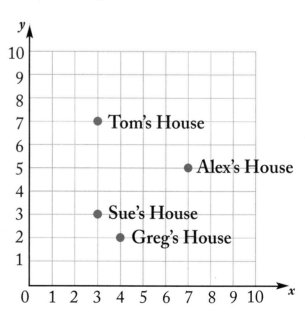

Name ______________________ Class __________ Date __________

20. Which of these numbers is the **smallest**?

Ⓐ 2,929

Ⓑ 3,100

Ⓒ 3,019

Ⓓ 2,986

21. What is the missing number in this pattern?

28, _____ , 20, 16

Ⓐ 32

Ⓑ 26

Ⓒ 24

Ⓓ 22

22. Paul's puppy is 24 months old. How many **years** is that?

Ⓐ 3 yr

Ⓑ 2 yr

Ⓒ $1\frac{1}{2}$ yr

Ⓓ 1 yr

Go On

23. Look at the figures below. Which two figures are **congruent**?

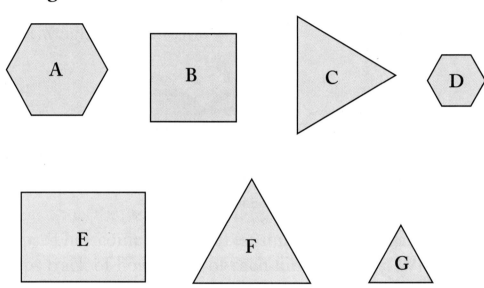

Ⓐ A and D

Ⓑ B and E

Ⓒ C and G

Ⓓ C and F

24. What number below can go in the blank to make this statement true?

1,153 < _____

Ⓐ 1,053

Ⓑ 1,135

Ⓒ 1,153

Ⓓ 1,183

25. Bag A contains $\frac{1}{2}$ pound of peanuts and $\frac{1}{2}$ pound of walnuts. How many pounds does the flour weigh?

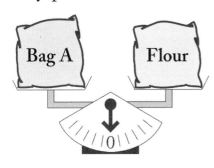

Ⓐ 5 lb

Ⓑ 3 lb

Ⓒ $2\frac{1}{2}$ lb

Ⓓ 1 lb

26. Look at these figures. What must you do to the figure on the left to get the figure on the right?

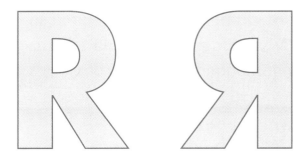

Ⓐ turn

Ⓑ turn and slide

Ⓒ flip

Ⓓ slide

27. Estimate 98×7. Which of the following numbers is closest to the actual answer?

    Ⓐ 600

    Ⓑ 700

    Ⓒ 800

    Ⓓ 900

28. Joan started at her house and walked to Frank's house. Which line graph shows her walking at a steady rate?

Ⓐ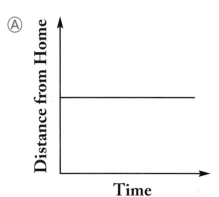

Ⓒ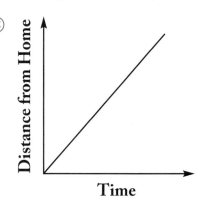

Ⓑ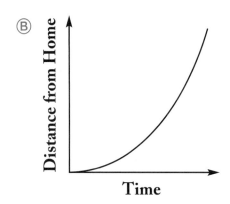

Ⓓ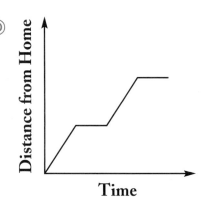

29. Look at the model below.

 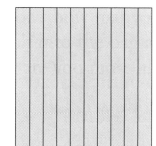 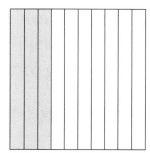

What mixed number is shown by the shaded parts?

Ⓐ $20\frac{2}{3}$

Ⓑ $20\frac{3}{10}$

Ⓒ $2\frac{2}{3}$

Ⓓ $2\frac{3}{10}$

30. Enrique has been reading about bridges. The Akashi Kaikyo Bridge in Japan is 12,828 feet long. The Golden Gate Bridge in California is 8,961 feet long. What operation must Enrique use to determine the difference in lengths?

Ⓐ addition

Ⓑ subtraction

Ⓒ multiplication

Ⓓ division

End of
Session 1

Session 2

Directions: There are 25 multiple-choice questions in this session. For each question, choose the best answer and mark your choice in the book.

31. Kristen looked in the pet shop window. These are the pets she saw in the window.

What fraction of the pets are **kittens**?

(A) $\frac{9}{2}$

(B) $\frac{1}{2}$

(C) $\frac{2}{7}$

(D) $\frac{2}{9}$

32. Raymond looks at the shapes below to see which shapes have parallel lines. Which of these shapes has **exactly two pairs** of parallel sides?

33. What number should go in the blank in order to make this number sentence true?

$(7 \times 6) + 2 = $ _____ $ + 2$

Ⓐ 35

Ⓑ 36

Ⓒ 42

Ⓓ 48

34. Joel has $50. He wants to buy as many T-shirts as he can. If each T-shirt costs $9, what is the **greatest** number of T-shirts he can buy?

Number of T-Shirts	1	2	3	4	5	6
Total Cost	$9	$18	$27	$36	$45	$54

Ⓐ 4 T-shirts

Ⓑ 5 T-shirts

Ⓒ 6 T-shirts

Ⓓ 7 T-shirts

35. Avi wants to buy some apples. The store sells bags with 8 apples in them. Avi buys 5 bags plus 3 more apples. Which expression shows how many apples Avi bought?

Ⓐ $8 \times (5 + 3)$

Ⓑ $8 + (5 \times 3)$

Ⓒ $(8 + 5) \times 3$

Ⓓ $(8 \times 5) + 3$

Name ______________________________ Class __________ Date __________

36. Bev makes a table of multiples of 6.

1	6
2	12
3	18
4	24
5	30
6	36
7	42
8	48

Which of the following statements is true about multiples of 6?

Ⓐ A multiple of 6 must end in an even number.

Ⓑ A multiple of 6 must be less than 100.

Ⓒ A multiple of 6 can end with any number.

Ⓓ A multiple of 6 must also be a multiple of 4.

37. Between which two numbers does 302 go?

Ⓐ between 150 and 299

Ⓑ between 275 and 410

Ⓒ between 303 and 489

Ⓓ between 457 and 621

Go On

38. Which tool should be used to measure the weight of a slice of bread?

Ⓐ a ruler

Ⓑ a compass

Ⓒ a thermometer

Ⓓ a scale

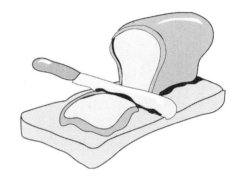

39. A brown paper bag contains

- 6 red marbles
- 3 yellow marbles
- 1 white marble

Maria picks one of the marbles from the bag without looking. What is the chance the marble will be **white**?

Ⓐ certain

Ⓑ not possible

Ⓒ least likely

Ⓓ most likely

40. Kelly is looking at a picture of her sister Gwen standing next to a flagpole. Gwen is about 5 feet tall. About how tall is the flagpole?

Ⓐ 10 ft

Ⓑ 25 ft

Ⓒ 50 ft

Ⓓ 75 ft

41. The perimeter of the figure below is 93 inches. What is the **length of side *DC*?**

Ⓐ 30 in.

Ⓑ 26 in.

Ⓒ 21 in.

Ⓓ 20 in.

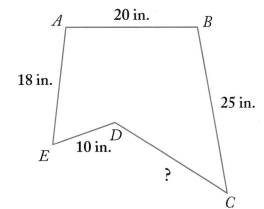

Go On

42. Find the missing factor that will make this number sentence true:

$8 \times \underline{\hspace{2em}} = 32$

Ⓐ 6

Ⓑ 5

Ⓒ 4

Ⓓ 3

43. Which is the **best estimate** for the height of a full-grown tree?

Ⓐ about 50 inches

Ⓑ about 4 feet

Ⓒ about 30 feet

Ⓓ about 2 miles

44. Which symbol should go in the blank in order to make this number sentence true?

30 inches _____ 3 feet

Ⓐ <

Ⓑ >

Ⓒ =

Ⓓ ÷

45. If Carl spins the spinner many times, on which letter will the arrow probably land **least** often?

Ⓐ Q

Ⓑ R

Ⓒ S

Ⓓ T

46. There are 16 eggs in Tanya's basket. Some of the eggs are brown. The rest of the eggs are white. There are **3 times** as many brown eggs as white eggs. How many eggs of each color are in the basket?

Ⓐ   6 brown eggs, 2 white eggs

Ⓑ 10 brown eggs, 6 white eggs

Ⓒ 12 brown eggs, 4 white eggs

Ⓓ 13 brown eggs, 3 white eggs

47. Which number is the **biggest**?

Ⓐ 25,100

Ⓑ 24,489

Ⓒ 24,917

Ⓓ 25,090

Go On

48. Erin has 2 bracelets and 2 rings. How many **different combinations** of 1 bracelet and 1 ring could she make?

Ⓐ 2

Ⓑ 4

Ⓒ 6

Ⓓ 8

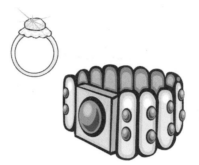 

49. Which of these figures has $\frac{1}{6}$ shaded?

Ⓐ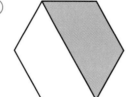

Ⓒ

Ⓑ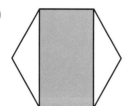

Ⓓ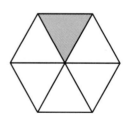

Name ________________________________ Class __________ Date __________

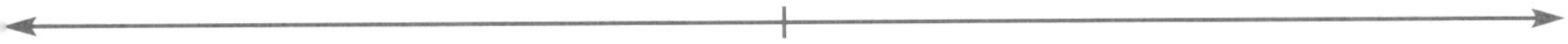

50. What missing number will make this number sentence true?

1,000 + _____ + 70 + 1 = 1,571

Ⓐ 5
Ⓑ 50
Ⓒ 500
Ⓓ 5,000

51. Which figure looks the same when turned 180 degrees?

Ⓐ 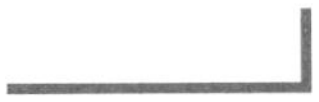

Ⓑ

Ⓒ

Ⓓ 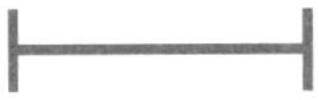

52. Tasha needs to wrap a small box. What units are the best ones to measure the box with?

Ⓐ millimeters
Ⓑ centimeters
Ⓒ meters
Ⓓ kilometers

Go On

53. The community pool is shaped like an L.

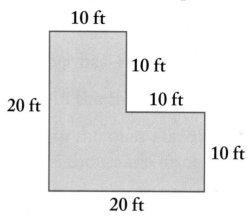

10 ft

10 ft

10 ft

20 ft

10 ft

20 ft

What is the perimeter of the pool?

Ⓐ   40 ft

Ⓑ   60 ft

Ⓒ   80 ft

Ⓓ 100 ft

54. Miguelito has 7 coins in his pocket. Their value in cents is as follows:

1, 1, 1, 5, 10, 10, and 25.

What is the **median** value?

Ⓐ 1

Ⓑ 5

Ⓒ 10

Ⓓ 25

55. Marisha put three 10-ounce blocks and one 1-ounce
block on the left side of her scale. Then she put
two 10-ounce blocks and three 1-ounce blocks on the
right. The scaled tipped to the left, so Marisha knew
the left side was heavier. What is the inequality shown
by the unbalanced scale?

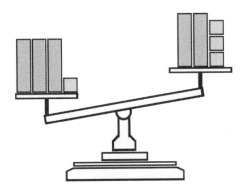

Ⓐ $3 \times 10 + 1 < 2 \times 10 + 3$

Ⓑ $3 \times 10 + 1 > 2 \times 10 + 3$

Ⓒ $3 \times (10 + 1) < 2 \times (10 + 3)$

Ⓓ $3 \times (10 + 1) > 2 \times (10 + 3)$

**End of
Session 2**

Appendix A: Mathematics Reference Sheet

NUMBERS

Cardinal Numbers

1	one
2	two
3	three
4	four
5	five
6	six
7	seven
8	eight
9	nine
10	ten

Ordinal Numbers

1st	first
2nd	second
3rd	third
4th	fourth
5th	fifth
6th	sixth
7th	seventh
8th	eighth
9th	ninth
10th	tenth

ABBREVIATIONS

Days

Sun.	Sunday
Mon.	Monday
Tues.	Tuesday
Wed.	Wednesday
Thurs.	Thursday
Fri.	Friday
Sat.	Saturday

Months

Jan.	January
Feb.	February
Mar.	March
Apr.	April
May	May
Jun.	June
Jul.	July
Aug.	August
Sept.	September
Oct.	October
Nov.	November
Dec.	December

Units

¢	cent
$	dollar
cm	centimeter
dm	decimeter
ft	foot
g	gram
in.	inch
kg	kilogram
km	kilometer
lb	pound
m	meter
mi	mile
mo	month
oz	ounce
T	ton
wk	week
yd	yard
yr	year

EQUIVALENTS

Time

1 year = 365 or 366 days
1 year = 12 months
1 year = 52 weeks + 1 or 2 days
1 week = 7 days
1 day = 24 hours
1 hour = 60 minutes
1 minute = 60 seconds

Weight

1 ton = 2,000 pounds
1 pound = 16 ounces

Length

1 yard = 3 feet
1 foot = 12 inches
1 meter = 100 centimeters

Appendix B: Rulers

You may cut out the rulers on this page and use them to help you answer questions about measuring.

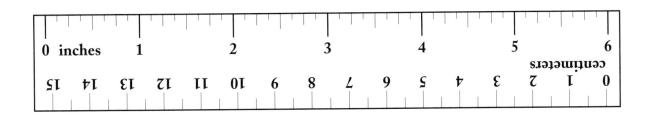

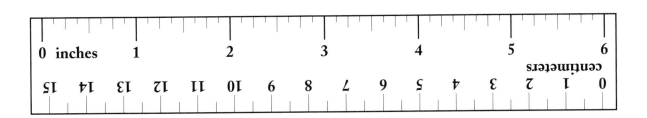

Appendix C: Diagnostic Test

Part 1: Basic Facts

1. $6 + 5 =$ _____

2. $11 - 6 =$ _____

3. $16 - 7 =$ _____

4. $9 - 5 =$ _____

5. $6 + 3 =$ _____

6. $17 - 8 =$ _____

7. $5 + 5 =$ _____

8. $9 + 7 =$ _____

9. $13 - 9 =$ _____

10. $5 \times 6 =$ _____

11. $4 \times 3 =$ _____

12. $11 - 9 =$ _____

13. $4 + 9 =$ _____

14. $5 + 6 =$ _____

15. $8 \times 3 =$ _____

16. $6 + 4 =$ _____

17. $12 - 7 =$ _____

18. $5 \times 3 =$ _____

19. $5 + 4 =$ _____

20. $3 \times 3 =$ _____

21. $10 - 7 =$ _____

22. $7 + 5 =$ _____

23. $4 + 8 =$ _____

24. $3 \times 5 =$ _____

25. $5 + 7 =$ _____

26. $3 \times 9 =$ _____

27. $4 + 7 =$ _____

28. $16 - 9 =$ _____

29. $8 + 6 =$ _____

30. $4 \times 5 =$ _____

31. $13 - 7 =$ _____

32. $3 + 9 =$ _____

33. $6 + 9 =$ _____

34. $6 \times 4 =$ _____

35. $8 + 7 =$ _____

36. $18 - 9 =$ _____

37. $14 - 8 =$ _____

38. $8 + 5 =$ _____

39. $9 - 6 =$ _____

40. $16 - 8 =$ _____

41. $9 - 9 =$ _____

42. $8 + 9 =$ _____

43. $6 + 7 =$ _____

44. $4 + 5 =$ _____

45. $14 - 7 =$ _____

46. $9 + 8 =$ _____

47. $9 + 4 =$ _____

48. $6 + 8 =$ _____

49. $7 \times 7 =$ _____

50. $13 - 6 =$ _____

51. $8 + 8 =$ _____

52. $7 + 3 =$ _____

53. $7 + 8 =$ _____

54. $5 + 8 =$ _____

55. $11 - 5 =$ _____

56. $4 \times 4 =$ _____

57. $5 + 9 =$ _____

58. $5 \times 5 =$ _____

59. $15 - 6 =$ _____

60. $3 + 8 =$ _____

Appendix C: Diagnostic Test (cont.)

Part 2: Basic Skills

Addition

1. $\begin{array}{r} 43 \\ +54 \\ \hline \end{array}$ $\qquad$ $\begin{array}{r} 35 \\ +29 \\ \hline \end{array}$ 2. $\begin{array}{r} 432 \\ +265 \\ \hline \end{array}$ $\qquad$ $\begin{array}{r} 385 \\ +667 \\ \hline \end{array}$

3. $\begin{array}{r} 18 \\ +30 \\ \hline \end{array}$ $\qquad$ $\begin{array}{r} 8 \\ +16 \\ \hline \end{array}$ 4. $\begin{array}{r} 5 \\ +8 \\ \hline \end{array}$ $\qquad$ $\begin{array}{r} 75 \\ +8 \\ \hline \end{array}$

Subtraction

1. $\begin{array}{r} 468 \\ -235 \\ \hline \end{array}$ $\qquad$ $\begin{array}{r} 423 \\ -286 \\ \hline \end{array}$ 2. $\begin{array}{r} 123 \\ -99 \\ \hline \end{array}$ $\qquad$ $\begin{array}{r} 285 \\ -63 \\ \hline \end{array}$

3. $\begin{array}{r} 624 \\ -323 \\ \hline \end{array}$ $\qquad$ $\begin{array}{r} 147 \\ -20 \\ \hline \end{array}$ 4. $\begin{array}{r} 325 \\ -151 \\ \hline \end{array}$ $\qquad$ $\begin{array}{r} 726 \\ -349 \\ \hline \end{array}$

Multiplication

1. $\begin{array}{r} 9 \\ \times 1 \\ \hline \end{array}$ $\qquad$ $\begin{array}{r} 9 \\ \times 2 \\ \hline \end{array}$ 2. $\begin{array}{r} 7 \\ \times 8 \\ \hline \end{array}$ $\qquad$ $\begin{array}{r} 8 \\ \times 7 \\ \hline \end{array}$

3. $\begin{array}{r} 6 \\ \times 5 \\ \hline \end{array}$ $\qquad$ $\begin{array}{r} 6 \\ \times 7 \\ \hline \end{array}$ 4. $\begin{array}{r} 8 \\ \times 2 \\ \hline \end{array}$ $\qquad$ $\begin{array}{r} 8 \\ \times 4 \\ \hline \end{array}$

Appendix D: Glossary

acute angle. An angle that measures less than 90°

addend. A number that is added in an addition problem

addition. An operation that puts numbers together. It is the opposite of subtraction. The answer is called the *sum*.

algorithm. A step-by-step process for solving a problem

alphabetical order. Arranged in the usual order of the letters of the alphabet

angle. The shape made by two rays that go out from a common endpoint. The angle is measured by the number of degrees between the rays.

area. The measurement of the space inside a flat shape

array. A rectangular arrangement of items in rows and columns

associative property of addition. A rule that states that the order in which numbers are grouped in an addition problem does not change the answer. Example: $(3 + 6) + 2 = 3 + (6 + 2)$

associative property of multiplication. A rule that states that the order in which numbers are grouped in a multiplication problem does not change the answer. Example: $(3 \times 6) \times 2 = 3 \times (6 \times 2)$

axis (plural: axes). A horizontal or vertical number line used in a graph

bar graph. A graph that uses bars to display data

base. Any side or face that a figure or shape can stand on without wobbling

capacity. The amount a container can hold

cardinal numbers. Numbers used to count. Examples: 1, 35, 872

Celsius scale. A scale for measuring temperature in which the freezing point of water is 0°C and the boiling point of water is 100°C

centimeter. A metric unit of length (abbreviated cm)

certain. Sure to happen

circle. A shape that is formed by connecting all the points at the same distance from its center

closed figure. A two-dimensional figure whose beginning and ending points meet. Examples: circle, square, rectangle

column graph. A bar graph that uses vertical bars to show amounts

commutative property of addition. A rule that states that the order of the numbers in an addition problem does not change the answer. Example: $3 + 6 = 6 + 3$

commutative property of multiplication. A rule that states that the order of the numbers in a multiplication problem does not change the answer. Example: $3 \times 6 = 6 \times 3$

cone. A three-dimensional figure with one curved surface, one vertex, and one circular base

congruent. Having the same size and shape

coordinate grid. A network of evenly spaced horizontal and vertical lines used for locating points or displaying data

coordinates. A pair of numbers that describes the location of a point on a grid

cube. A rectangular prism that has six square faces

cubic unit. A measure of volume that is 1 unit by 1 unit by 1 unit

cup. A customary unit of capacity (abbreviated c). There are 2 cups in a pint and 4 cups in a quart.

customary units. Units of measurement used in the United States, such as inch, foot, cup, and pound. See also *metric system.*

cylinder. A three-dimensional shape with one curved surface and two circular bases

data. Facts, or a collection of information, on a subject

day. A unit of time equal to 24 hours

decimal point. A dot that separates dollars from cents or whole numbers from tenths, hundredths, etc.

decimeter. A metric unit of length (abbreviated dm)

degree. A unit of measurement for temperature or an angle

denominator. The bottom part of a fraction. It tells the amount of the whole or the total number in the group.

diagonal. A line segment that connects two vertices of a polygon

diameter. The distance across a circle through its center

difference. The answer in a subtraction problem

digits. The single numbers 0, 1, 2, 3, 4, 5, 6, 7, 8, and 9.

dimensions. Length, width, and height

discrete math. Mathematics about things that can be counted

distributive property of multiplication over addition. A rule that states that multiplying a number by the sum of two addends gives the same result as multiplying the number by each addend and adding the products. Example: $4(3 + 2) = (4 \times 3) + (4 \times 2)$

dividend. The number to be divided in a division problem. Example: $8 \div 4 = 2$. The dividend is 8.

division. An operation that tells how many times a number can go into another number. It is the reverse operation of multiplication. The answer is called the *quotient.*

divisor. The number by which a dividend is divided. Example: $8 \div 4 = 2$. The divisor is 4.

dozen. Twelve

endpoint. The point from which a ray extends, or the ends of a line segment

equal. The same

equally likely. Having the same chance of happening

equals sign. The symbol =, which means that the values on both sides of the symbol are the same

equation. A number sentence that uses the equals sign (=) to show that two amounts are the same

equilateral triangle. A triangle with three equal sides and three equal angles (60°)

equivalent. An amount that is equal to another amount but given in different units

equivalent fractions. Fractions that have different numerators and denominators but equal the same amount

estimate. To find a number that is close to an exact answer

even. Able to be divided by 2 without a remainder. Examples: 0, 2, 4, 6

face. A flat surface of a three-dimensional figure

fact family. Related addition and subtraction facts or multiplication and division facts that use the same numbers

factor. A number that is multiplied in a multiplication problem; a whole number that can be divided evenly into another whole number

Fahrenheit scale. A scale for measuring temperature in which the freezing point of water is 32°F and the boiling point of water is 212°F

flip. A transformation that produces the mirror image of a figure

fluid ounce. A customary unit of capacity (abbreviated fl oz). There are 8 fluid ounces in 1 cup.

foot. A customary unit of length (abbreviated ft). One foot equals 12 inches.

fraction. A part of a whole. Example: $\frac{1}{4}$ means 1 part out of 4.

front-end estimation. A method for estimating using only the front (first) digit of each number

gallon. A customary unit of capacity (abbreviated gal). One gallon is equal to 4 quarts or 8 pints or 16 cups.

geometric figures. Two- or three-dimensional shapes. Examples: circle, square, cone, pyramid

gram. A metric unit of mass (abbreviated g)

graph. A picture that shows data in an organized way

greater than. The symbol >, which means that the value on the left of the symbol is larger than the value on the right

grid. Evenly spaced horizontal and vertical lines

horizontal. Running left to right

hour. A unit of time (abbreviated hr)

identity property for addition. A rule that states that adding a zero in an addition problem does not change the sum. Example: 4 + 0 = 4

identity property for multiplication. A rule that states that multiplying a number by 1 gives that number

impossible. Something that cannot happen

inequality. A number sentence that states that one side is greater than, greater than or equal to, less than, or less than or equal to the other side. Examples: $3 + 2 < 6$; $5 - x \geq 1$

intersecting lines. Lines that meet or cross one another

isosceles triangle. A triangle that has two sides of equal length and two equal angles

kilogram. A metric unit of mass (abbreviated kg)

kilometer. A metric unit of length (abbreviated km)

length. A measure of the distance between the ends of something

less likely. Having a smaller chance of happening

less than. The symbol <, which means that the value on the left of the symbol is smaller than the value on the right

likelihood. The chance that something will happen. See *equally likely, less likely, more likely,* and *probability.*

line. A set of points extending forever in opposite directions. A line has one dimension—length.

line graph. A graph that displays data points along a line

line of symmetry. A line that divides a figure into two congruent shapes

line segment. See *segment.*

liter. A metric unit of capacity (abbreviated L). One liter is equal to 1000 milliliters.

mass. The amount of stuff in an object

measure. To find how long, how heavy, or how big something is

median. The middle number of a set of numbers arranged in order

meter. A metric unit of length (abbreviated m)

metric system. A system for measurement used in most of the world and based on 10. See also *customary units.*

milliliter. A metric unit of capacity (abbreviated mL). There are 1000 milliliters in 1 liter.

minuend. In a subtraction problem, the number that is taken away. Example: In $5 - 3 = 2$, the minuend is 3.

minute. A unit of time (abbreviated min). There are 60 seconds in 1 minute and 60 minutes in 1 hour.

mode. The data point that occurs most often in a set of data

month. A unit of time (abbreviated mo). There are 12 months in 1 year.

more likely. Having a greater chance of happening

multiples. Numbers that result from multiplying a given number by each whole number. Example: Some multiples of 15 are 15, 30, 45, 60, and 75.

multiplication. An operation that simplifies adding the same number many times. It is the opposite of division. The answer is called the *product.*

number line. A line with evenly spaced numbers that shows the order of numbers

numerator. The top part in a fraction. It refers to parts of the whole or the portion of the group.

obtuse angle. An angle that measures more than 90°

octagon. A flat shape with 8 sides

odd. The numbers 1, 3, 5, 7, and so on

operation. A mathematical process, such as addition or division

ordinal numbers. Numbers that show order. Examples: first (1st), fifty-third (53rd)

organized list. Data that is arranged and displayed in a meaningful way

ounce. A customary unit of weight (abbreviated oz). There are 16 ounces in 1 pound.

paired numbers. A set of two numbers related to one another in such a way that if you know the rule for the relationship and either one of the numbers, you can find the other number

parallel lines. Lines in the same plane that do not cross. They are the same distance apart everywhere along the lines.

parallelogram. A four-sided flat figure with two pairs of parallel sides. Its opposite sides are equal, and its opposite angles are equal.

pattern. A predictable sequence of numbers or objects that repeat or follow a set plan

perimeter. The sum of the lengths of all the sides of a polygon

period. In a number, a group of three digits set off by commas. When you read a number, you read the place values for each group, followed by the period name, such as "thousand."

perpendicular lines. Lines that meet or cross at a right angle (90°)

pictograph. A graph that uses symbols to show data

pint. A customary unit of capacity (abbreviated pt). There are 2 pints in 1 quart.

place value. The value assigned to the position of a digit in a number

place-value chart. A chart that shows the place values of all the digits in a number. The places can represent whole numbers, such as ones and tens, or decimals, such as tenths and hundredths.

plot. To mark the location of a point on a graph or coordinate grid

point. A single spot in space. A point has no dimensions (no length, width, or height).

polygon. A flat, closed figure formed by straight lines that do not cross

possible. Able to happen

pound. A customary unit of weight (abbreviated lb). One pound equals 16 ounces.

predict. Use what you know to tell what might happen

prism. A three-dimensional figure with bases that are congruent and parallel and sides that are parallelograms

probability. The chance that something will happen

product. The answer in a multiplication problem

properties. Rules that numbers follow. Example: commutative property

pyramid. A solid shape with only one base. The other faces are triangles.

quadrilateral. A closed figure with 4 sides

quart. A customary unit of capacity (abbreviated qt). One quart equals 2 pints or 4 cups.

quotient. The answer in a division problem

range. The difference between the highest number and the lowest number in a data set

ray. A portion of a line that begins at a point and goes on forever in one direction. An angle is formed when two rays are joined at their endpoints.

reasonable. Close to the estimated value for an answer

rectangle. A quadrilateral with opposite sides that are equal and four right angles

rectangular prism. A prism whose faces are all rectangles

regroup. In column addition, subtraction, or multiplication, to rename part of the value of one place and move it to another place to make the operation easier. Example: 53 is the same as 4 tens and 13 ones.

remainder. In a division problem, the amount left over after the division is done. Example: If you divide 3 into 13, the quotient is 4 and the remainder is 1.

represent. To stand for or take the place of

rhombus. A four-sided flat figure with sides that are all the same length. The opposite sides are parallel.

right angle. An angle that makes a square corner. It measures exactly 90°.

right triangle. A triangle that contains a right angle

rotate. To turn a figure around a point

rounding. Changing an exact number into another number that is close to its value and easier to work with

rule. A mathematical fact that describes a pattern or relationship

scalene triangle. A triangle with all three sides of different lengths

scales. The numbers given to the axes of a graph or the units of measure on a ruler or a thermometer

second. A unit of time (abbreviated sec). There are 60 seconds in 1 minute.

segment. A portion of a line that has a beginning and an end

set. A group of items

slide. A transformation that moves an object or shape across a surface

solve. To find the answer to a problem or find a number that makes an equation true

sphere. A three-dimensional shape with one curved surface—no edges, bases, or vertices. Every point is the same distance from the center.

square. A four-sided polygon with four right angles and four sides that are the same length

square foot. A customary unit of area that is one foot by one foot

square meter. A metric unit of area that is one meter by one meter

square pyramid. A pyramid whose base is a square

square unit. A unit of area that is one unit by one unit in size

standard form. The usual way of writing a number using digits and place value

straight angle. An angle that measures 180°. It looks like a straight line.

subtraction. An operation that takes away numbers. It is the opposite of addition. The answer is called the *difference.*

subtrahend. In a subtraction problem, the number from which something is taken away. Example: In 5 − 3 = 2, the number 5 is the subtrahend.

sum. The answer to an addition problem

symbol. A sign that stands for something

symmetry. A characteristic of a shape such that one half is the mirror image of the other

table. A chart that organizes and shows information about a topic

tally. To keep count by making marks. Example: These tally marks show the number 4: ||||.

temperature. The measure of the amount of heat in an object

tessellation. A repeating pattern of shapes that fit together with no spaces in between

three-dimensional figure. A figure that takes up space and has volume. Its dimensions are length, width, and height. Examples: cube and cylinder

transformations. Changes made to a shape through slides, turns, and flips

trapezoid. A four-sided polygon with only two sides that are parallel

tree diagram. A diagram showing all possible outcomes of an event

triangle. A polygon with three sides and three angles

triangular prism. A prism whose bases are triangles

triangular pyramid. A pyramid whose base is a triangle

turn. A change made to a figure by rotating it around a point

two-dimensional figure. A shape with two dimensions—length and width. A two-dimensional shape does not have thickness.

unit. A fixed quantity used to measure

value. What something is worth, or the amount that it stands for

Venn diagram. A way to show how groups of items are related by putting members of each group into a circle. Items that are in the area where the circles overlap are in both groups.

vertex (plural: vertices). The point at which two sides of an angle meet in a figure

vertical. Running up and down

volume. The amount of space taken up by a solid

week. A unit of time (abbreviated wk). One week is equal to 7 days.

weight. How heavy an object is, or how strongly it is pulled down by gravity

whole number. The numbers in the set {0, 1, 2, 3, …}.

year. A unit of time (abbreviated yr). There are 12 months in 1 year.

zero property of multiplication. A rule that states that the product of any number and 0 is 0. Example: $4 \times 0 = 0$ and $0 \times 4 = 0$.

Index

L

leap year, 91
length, 153–154, 157–158, 161
less likely, 213
less than (<), 63
likely, 213
line(s), 123; intersecting, 124; parallel, 124; perpendicular, 124; segment, 123; of symmetry, 139–140
line graphs, 114, 205–206
line of symmetry, 139–140
liter (L), 173

M

mass, 177–178
measuring, 153; area, 165–166; capacity, 173–174; length, 153–154, 157–158; mass, 177–178; perimeter, 161–162; temperature, 185–186; time, 181–182; volume, 169–170; weight, 177–178
median, 210
meter (m), 157
metric units, 157–158; of area, 165; of capacity, 173; of length, 157; of mass, 177; of volume, 169
milliliter (mL), 173
Minard, Charles Joseph, 197
minuend, 68
minute, 181
mirror image, 140, 148
mode, 209
money, 189–192
month, 181
more likely, 213
multiple-choice questions, 32
multiplication, 79–80, 83–84; fact family, 88; vocabulary for, 54

N

Newton, Sir Isaac, 177
number(s), paired, 109–110, 113
number line, 64, 68, 91
number sentence, 117
number(s), 59; cardinal, 261; comparing and ordering, 63–64, 100; even, 90; fractions, 99; odd, 90; ordinal, 261; properties of, 67, 80; rounding, 91–92; standard form for, 60; whole, 63; word names for, 60
numerator, 99

O

obtuse angle, 124
octagon, 127
odd, 90
operation symbols, 117
ordinal numbers, 261
organized list, 217
origami, 135
ounce (oz), 178

P

paired numbers, 109–110, 113
parallel lines, 124
parallelogram, 128
Pascal, Blaise, 75
pattern(s), 46, 56, 105–106, 109–110
perimeter, 161–162
period, 59
perpendicular lines, 124
pictographs, 201–202
pint (pt), 173–174
place value, 59–60; chart, 59, 63; models, 76, 83, 92
plot, 144

symbol, 201
symmetry, 139–140; line of, 139–140

T

table, 109, 110, 197
temperature, 185–186
tessellations, 150
test-taking tips, 35–38
test-taking words, 56
thermometer, 185–186
Thompson, LaMarcus, 147
three-dimensional shapes, 131–132, 169;
   cone, 131; cube, 131; cylinder, 131;
   prisms, 131; pyramids, 131; sphere, 131
time, 181–182
ton (T), 178
transformation(s), 147–148; flip, 148; slide,
   147; turn, 147
trapezoid, 128
tree diagram, 218
triangle(s), 127, 128; equilateral, 128;
   isosceles, 128; right, 128; scalene, 128
triangular prism, 131
triangular pyramid, 131
turn, 147
two-dimensional shapes, 127–128, 169;
   circle, 127; quadrilateral, 127, 128;
   triangle, 127, 128

U

unit, 153

V

value, 59
Venn diagram, 217, 219–220
Venn, John, 217
vertex, 123, 134
vertical, 143
volume, 169–170

W

Warhol, Andy, 136
weather forecasting, 214
week, 181
weight, 177–178
whole numbers, 63
width, 161
word name, 60
word problems, 39–40, 43–48

X

x-axis, 205

Y

y-axis, 205
yard (yd), 153
year, 181

Z

zero property of multiplication, 80